Passion Won't Pay the Bills

PASSION WON'T PAY THE BILLS

10 Mistakes that Close Youth-Serving Programs
& What You Can Do to Thrive

LINETTE M. DANIELS, Ph. D.

EYS Publishing ✦ Midlothian, VA

Published by EYS Publishing
Midlothian, VA

Cover Design and Interior Layout by Imagine! Studios™
www.artsimagine.com

ISBN 13: 978-0-9834232-3-2

LCCN: 2011927643

First EYS Publishing printing, May 2011

*This book is dedicated to all the youth
program leaders who tirelessly serve in the
trenches every day . . . celebrating, motivating
and empowering youth for success.*

*"You are writing the story of a child's life one day at
a time; I challenge you to Make It A Happy Ending! "*

Contents

Introduction

I am Linette Daniels also known as the Youth Success Doctor. Allow me to tell you a little bit about myself. I am a national speaker, author and success strategist who, for the past 20 years, has empowered youth from the cradle through college in a variety of youth-serving arenas to include public school, child care, foster care, juvenile court, social services, and early intervention.

I've owned several for profit youth-serving businesses—to include three child care centers which were open 24 hours a day, 7 days a week—and founded a 501(c) (3) non-profit organization. As a single parent, I raised 12 therapeutic foster care and 2 biological children using my vision to see infants' progress into developmentally strong toddlers, academically prepared preschoolers, empowered youth and successful adults. I also love teaching kids how to start a business so I do a lot of work with youth entrepreneurs.

As you can see, I truly have a heart for youth empowerment. It is my life's purpose but I cannot do it alone.

It IS going to take a village to empower youth for success and building that tribe has become the focus for the next phase of my life.

I have spent the last 20 years or more helping people start and run a successful business. I have helped large organizations like Big Brothers/Big Sisters and the Boys & Girls Club. I've helped some smaller youth-serving organizations like Team-Up Richmond and The Teen Toolbox. I am passionate about coaching the Growth, Programming & Sustainability of Youth-Serving Programs because *I believe that given the right space, tools, and training; ALL youth can succeed.*

As CEO of Empowering Youth for Success, I am on a mission to see youth excel in business, master money and be great leaders so they can create the life they want to live. As founder of the International Association of Youth-Empowerment Programs (IAYEP), my mission is to show youth-serving CEO's, Founders and Directors how to build a heart-centered program that also generates income so you can focus on empowering more youth. I know you are not in this for the money but "Passion Won't Pay The Bills".

I look forward to sharing this journey with you. I have found that youth-serving businesses can be difficult to get off the ground so my goal is to make youth program success easier. It doesn't have to be hard and you certainly do not have to travel the road alone. I have been where you are and unfortunately many of the things I am going to tell you, I had to learn the hard way. Just like raising kids, there is no manual on how to run a successful youth-serving program, and when I started my businesses there was no Internet and no expert consultant teaching what I know now. I had to learn through trial and lots of error.

You can have a heart-centered program that makes money. I did it and so can you.

Through this book, I am going to share the secret to my success. I am going to talk about how and what it will take to achieve the success you desire. Whether you are thinking about starting a youth program, have a brand new program or have been in business for years, this book will be beneficial. Perhaps you have a child care center, a skill building organization or mentoring program and things are not quite the way you would like them to be. Maybe you are already successful in your business but having a difficult time pushing through the ceiling to the next level or you could still be stuck in a J-O-B because it is financing your passion. Regardless of where you fall on the continuum, my 6 Pillars to Success System is the same for everyone; you will just use the pillars in a slightly different way.

I am so excited for the opportunity to be your guide in creating the youth-serving program of your dreams. I have a lot to share so I recommend you get a binder and take notes on what you read in this book. There are many ways to use the information and having a notebook will aid you in brainstorming as we go along.

So let's jump right in and get started!

For the sake of making the information an easy read, beginning with chapter two each chapter will cover one pillar of success. The first pillar is Branding, followed by Clarity, Marketing, Visibility, Programming, and Sustainability. I encourage you to read over each chapter until you fully understand the concept I am explaining. The 6 Pillars are essentially puzzle pieces where you may not get the complete picture until all six pillars are in place.

It is not uncommon for me to issue challenges throughout the book. The challenges will be directly related to the concepts

I share and is designed to help you fully develop your understanding, and support implementation of the 6 Pillars.

Now that you have an overview of the chapters to come, let the journey begin.

1

10 Mistakes That Close Youth-Serving Programs

Do you have what it takes to be a successful youth-serving executive?

Statistics have shown that 95% of all new businesses bail out within the first few years. This is due to the realization that owning and operating a business is more difficult than it initially seems. Perhaps you fall into this category. In my 20+ years of experience working with youth-serving programs, I have seen this first hand. I have seen youth-serving programs flourish while others flounder. What I deem significant about the failures of youth-serving programs is not *how* the businesses failed but how they handled the failure once it occurred. The fact of the matter is, not all business are successful the first go around. It sometimes takes two or even three times to get the business functioning properly. Think about it. If success were easy, everyone would have it! To be a successful youth-serving program, begin by studying why other programs have failed and be determined not to follow in the same path. No matter how long it takes to succeed, look at your failures and the failures of businesses similar to yours as a learning experience. These experiences can be used as your stepping stone to success.

If failure is inevitable for so many, what causes it?

Through my experience with youth-serving programs, I have noticed time and time again several reasons why programs fail. Allow me to share the top 10 reasons with you.

1. CHANGING EMOTIONS, CHANGES SUCCESS.

Youth program executives have many things in common, especially in your character. You are generally passionate, courageous, optimistic, independent, enthusiastic, and have a desire to help young people. You can be described as visionaries with a slew of powerful, positive emotions. While these are all great emotions, these very emotions can have a devastating impact on your program's success. Many heart centered people allow their emotions to guide decisions which affect the business negatively. An example of this is not being open to ideas and suggestion for change or improvement because you are emotionally tied to your original business idea. While it is not wrong to have emotions, one *must* recognize these emotions and act in a manner that will benefit the business. If you let your emotions control your thoughts and actions your business will suffer.

Being disciplined in completing your vision is critical. The lack of discipline leads to wasted talent. Many youth-serving executives are just not disciplined enough to put in the work required to make the business a success. If you are really doing what you are passionate about, then make the decision to do the work. Working towards your goal should give you joy. If it does not, perhaps you have a hobby rather than a business. If you find yourself having a discipline problem when it comes to business, take time to step back and examine what you really want out of life. Is it truly to have a successful business? If not, you may want to consider an alternative route. I'm reminded of a quote by H. Jackson Brown Jr. that says "Talent without discipline is like an octopus on roller skates. There's plenty of movement, but you never know if it's going to be forward, backs wards or sideways." You must know where you are going with your business and how you plan to get there.

2. PLAN, PLAN, PLAN, AND PLAN SOME MORE.

While some youth-serving executives have trouble finding a single direction for their program, others know exactly what it takes to get the program up and running. They have taken the time to prepare and have business plans that address every possible detail. The problem arises when you fail to take action to get things done. It is not enough to be a great planner when creating a youth-serving program; you must know how to market your program or service. For many heart-centered executives the thought of marketing can lead to feelings of fear, dread, uncertainty, and regret. If you find yourself in this position, consider getting a coach or consultant to help you take action and provide positive support as each step is taken. A coach who is knowledgeable about youth-serving programs can motivate you to carry out your plan and aide in your program success.

3. LEAPING BEFORE YOU LOOK.

Opening your youth-serving program before you have adequately planned can also lead to failure. If you rush to open your doors, important steps can get overlooked. Failure to plan can lead to poor execution. If a viable market is overlooked or your program has too much competition, your business will not thrive. Having the correct pricing strategy is pertinent to the success of your program as well. Poor decisions can occur as a direct result of poor planning. Failure to thoroughly plan each and every aspect of your business will negatively affect its sustainability.

4. IDEAS NEED MONEY TO SPEND.

One of the biggest hurdles youth-serving executives face is finding the resources needed for success. How will you support yourself while you're growing the program? How much capital will you need to get started? Have you evaluated all of the costs in running the business including—paying employees, buying or leasing space, etc? Many businesses fail because they underestimate the start-up costs and the length of time it will take to generate revenue.

Many youth-serving executives also fail because they enter the market with a scarcity mindset. This can be dangerous to your business. It is important to enter the business world with a positive energy toward money. Competition or even the thought of it has the potential to destroy your business. Try to have the mindset that money is in abundance to support your vision.

In contrast to the scarcity mindset and just as dangerous to your program success is starting too big. If you use too much leverage in your company, you can bankrupt it quickly. When beginning your youth-serving program consider keeping costs low. Use equity capital to finance your business. Avoid fixed obligations until you are established. You want to have a mass of customers before you take your company to a higher level of expenses. This can be in the form of renting a larger space or hiring staff. Whatever the expense, make sure you have established your program as a key player in the market before you assume unnecessary debt.

5. FOLLOWING BRIGHT SHINY OBJECTS.

As a youth-program executive, you must develop single minded focus and determination. You need to know what you want to accomplish and focus on it until you succeed. Having clarity will determine whether your program is a success or failure. Picking one thing to focus on will keep you from being mentally scattered. Once you have chosen your focus, you need to write measurable goals and be persistent in meeting those goals. If you do not have the dedication to keep going, you will likely fail. Most youth-serving programs close because they simply give up. Remember, it will take hard work, persistence, and dedication. A friend once told me he failed 3 or 4 times just to make sure he had everything right. You must train yourself emotionally for the lows and highs that come with any business. Running a successful youth-serving program is like training for a marathon. Each time you fail it will get easier and easier.

6. IF IT LOOKS LIKE A HOBBY AND ACTS LIKE A HOBBY . . .

You will hear me say time and time again that passion won't pay the bills. Many youth-serving programs fail because executives do not understand they are running a business. While it is true that having a passion for youth can increase your success – passion is not all you need. You must dedicate time and effort to developing your services and other aspects of your business that may not come naturally to you. If you are not marketing and selling, the doors of your program are destined to close.

Youth-serving programs must have integrity and be reliable. Meeting deadlines and following through is a necessity in business. If you cannot keep your commitments, you will not be trusted. Consumers are looking for someone they can trust with their child's health, safety and welfare. Operating your program like a business will go a long way to building a trusting relationship with your customers.

7. FOE SUPPORT OR NO SUPPORT.

Many youth-serving programs fail because of pure selfishness. You will go broke if you try to be a one-man show. Don't fall into the trap of thinking you can do everything yourself. You need other people to help make your business a success. Givers usually end up earning more. Don't be selfish with your business. You *will* need help if you want your program to grow. Consider having someone complete part-time bookkeeping and administrative tasks. An accountant can also be useful for tax purposes. Once you develop relationships with key people you will gain the motivational and emotional support needed for your business endeavors. A good team will want to see your business succeed, too.

Having no support will slow your growth to a snail's pace but having internal discord can completely destroy your program. Some youth-serving programs fail in the beginning because of mangled business relationships. Starting a business can be stressful and disagreements about the direction of the organization can lead to a rift among team members. Structure agreements will ensure that founders and key hires are treated fairly and everyone's interests are closely aligned with the goals of the program. Operating a successful business will require getting out of your comfort zone and this will hold true for the team you choose to support your vision. Avoid alignments with people who bring you down or negatively impact your business.

8. WHAT YOU DON'T KNOW WILL CLOSE YOU.

One of the top 10 reasons youth-serving programs fail is your lack of knowledge in the area of marketing. A marketing plan needs to be developed, measured as it is carried out, and revised as needed. How will you get your message out? Sadly, many youth-serving executives do not fully understand how to properly market their program. They are not up to date on the vast array of marketing tools and resources available – such as social media. Where do you get this knowledge? Reading this book is a great start but three of the top ways to stay current on the best program resources is by attending conferences, joining a youth-serving association and reading industry publications. Many executives do not spend the time or money to obtain knowledge—but it is less expensive than bankruptcy.

Similar to having a lack of knowledge in marketing, is not realizing that competing head-to-head with industry leaders will be difficult. A sure sign of impending failure is a youth-serving entrepreneur who plans to bootstrap his new business while competing directly against established youth-serving programs. Large programs have enormous resources to deter competitors from entering the playing field. They can undercut your prices, outspend you on advertising, and choke off access to suppliers and distributors. I strongly advise against making a frontal assault unless you have a world-class team and very deep pockets. Even then, your chances of success are likely to be disappointing. Consider offering a service unavailable at larger youth-serving programs—offering a service other programs do not have can skyrocket your business but only when it's what your prospective clients want. There is no success in being a market of one!

Beware of growing too fast. This, too, can lead to failure. Uncontrolled growth can kill youth-serving programs by not having an infrastructure that allows the business to scale properly. Growth often requires additional investments in fixed assets and working capital—so be sure to create a plan for growth. At controlled rates of growth, your program can handle incremental increases in expenses. Hyper-growth can suck up large amounts of cash forcing your business into debt or bringing the whole program to a screeching halt. Focusing solely on profitability rather than cash flow can lead to business collapse.

9. GETTING LOST IN THE WILDERNESS!

You may be wondering why you are spending so much time and energy trying to get your youth-serving program going or growing. This is a common feeling among business owners and grassroots program executives—who are working too hard *in* the program rather than *on* the program. It is easy to get caught up in operating details rather than seeking strategies and systems for increased success. If you find yourself in this situation—focus on why you want to help youth and how much they will benefit from the program or service you offer. Most importantly, determine whether or not you have strayed away from your original vision. Exploring these areas can revive the pulse of your program. Consider creating a vision and a mission statement to keep you on track as well as provide visual support when times get tough.

10. YOU'RE GETTING OLDER, BUT NOT BETTER.

Many youth-serving programs fail because the executive refuses to invest in themselves. It is important to realize that many people will be affected if you don't face what is not going well in your business. If you are spending so much time in your program that you do not have time for others—emotionally, physically, spiritually, and financially—your business will suffer. Know where you need to make changes and do what it takes to improve your business and still have a life. Beyond the youth empowerment knowledge needed to run your program, you need to also grow personally. Creating a successful youth-serving program will not be an easy task but you must maintain a healthy balance between your business and personal life.

There you have it. The top 10 reasons youth-serving programs fail. I encourage you to grade yourself in each area and where you rate less than 'B'—seek additional knowledge and create a plan for improvement. With the correct guidance your program can succeed beyond your wildest dreams and the remainder of this book will show you how.

2

Success Pillar #1: Branding

irst and foremost, you need to understand what you are. I want us to be on the same page upfront because I know it is a struggle for many youth-serving executives to see the program as a business. Whether you are a youth-serving organization, program, or government agency—you are running a business. Whether you are for-profit or not-for-profit—you are still a business. I am going to use the word *business* often so it can sink in because until you wrap your mind around that— you are definitely going to struggle with programming, sustainability, and growth.

Often times I hear people say "I already know my brand" or "I am fine with my brand". But there is more to branding that you may think. It is important to know that a brand is so much more than a name, logo, or tag line. A brand is a perception that the market has about your company, your product, or your service. And truthfully, whether you like it or not, your business has a brand and that brand is based on what the public thinks about your business. The "public" includes customers, prospective customers, and business associates, as well as any staff you may have. Fortunately, if you have a business or are thinking about starting a youth-serving business, it is never too late to give yourself a brand or a brand facelift. You may need to scrap your brand and start fresh. But that's okay. If you're willing to put in the work you can create an awesome brand that will draw customers and give you the future success you intended your program to have.

Let's talk about four general areas you can use to brand your business so it's just the way you want it to be. Remember, if you have a business, you have a brand whether you have purposely created that brand or not.

PUBLIC IMAGE

Every company or product has an image but not every image is the one you want. If you have given your customer the power to create your imagine, it is important to take back the reins over what people think and say about your program. Many times, what customers say is not necessarily negative but it may be totally different than what you want your image to be.

What do you want your *program* to be known for?

What do *you* want to be known for?

Your response to those two questions is what your brand should indicate. Again, I emphasize, do not let your customer dictate your brand.

Branding can be much like nicknaming. When we were in school it was not uncommon for a friend to give us a nickname. Many times it was a nickname that you did not like; however, it was a nickname based on *their* physical, social or psychological perception of you. I'm going to share something with you that I have not thought about in years—so this is our little secret, okay? When I was young, my nickname was *Cleopatra Bones* because I was skinny as a beanpole. My friends didn't choose a name that had to do with beauty or brains. They picked what was foremost in their mind about me—which is very similar to what happens when clients brand your business. This is not the way you want to be branded and something you may quickly need to change if it has.

Is your business branded the way you want to be remembered?

Do you even know what your customers say about your business behind your back?

That's exactly what you need to think about when it comes to *branding* and *public image.* You may know what you want people to think, but is that what they see? Is that what they remember? When a current or a potential customer thinks about your business, they may believe you are an established leader in your industry—or they could be thinking you're a strong number two. They may think you are the most experienced in your industry—or that you're a new player with potential. They could be thinking you're good with small clients—or you only work with larger clients. They might also think you offer the most reliable product, service or program—or they may think you offer the best product, service, or program. They might believe that you offer premium quality—or you're the cheap alternative when they can't afford the best.

> ### FREEZE
>
> This last example is a big deal because when it comes to serving youth, you really can't afford to be seen as the cheap alternative. But let's face it; especially if you are a child care center, an after-school program or any service where you physically monitor children—parents tend to choose based on price. You do not want to be in the money battle. You don't want your brand to be "the cheapest program" because trust me, if your program is the best and you are branding yourself that way—the parents won't care that you are also the most expensive.

The list of branding examples could go on and on but when it's all said and done—whether positive or negative—there is going to be at least one adjective that comes to mind when your customer thinks about your program. So ask yourself, what are my business strengths and what do I want my business to be known for? If clients are going to choose an element to remember, you should be the one behind the driver's seat.

As great as your services and programs may be, eventually, you're going to have a customer you just cannot satisfy. That customer will probably shout a whole lot louder about their dissatisfaction than all the other customers who are very happy with your service. If you leave your brand up to your customers—you have no idea what you may get. If your program is the best—your clients will know because your brand says so. I'll talk about branding more as we go along.

Your public image is essential to branding so make sure you develop a plan for creating your brand rather than letting your clients create it for you.

BUSINESS PLAN

The next tool or area we need to discuss in branding is a *business plan.* You absolutely should have a written business plan that speaks to your values and the image you want to portray. When it comes to working with young people, you need to examine your personal image as well as the image of your business. Understand that you cannot separate *your* image from your business image. You would have to be humongous like *Coca Cola* before you will drift into the woodwork and people only see the brand you've created. I don't know who owns *Coca Cola* and I don't care. As a result of Coke having such a strong brand, when I go to the store I'm thinking "Coke is great!" and I'm looking for the red and white can. But because most youth-serving programs are much smaller, anything *you* do is going to also reflect on your business.

Your business plan is the roadmap that guides everything you do and every business decision you make. You want to ask yourself, *does my idea match or further the brand I'm trying to build?* Maybe it's an idea for a new service. Maybe it's collaborating with another program. Maybe it was the idea to buy this book. Your question should always be, *does the idea match or further my brand?* And if it doesn't—you don't need to do it. Please hear me. Every good idea doesn't have to be done by you. I know this is a real challenge in the youth-serving market because we have such huge hearts but you must stay true to your business plan and what you want your business to be about. I struggled with this for a long time. Being helpful is our kryptonite so on occasion, I still struggle. Let me share what I've learned to do and what I believe will help you too. I located, I studied, and I searched for experts in my field who offer a variety of other services. If someone has a problem that is not part of my brand—I quickly refer them to resources that can help. You can be helpful without being "the" source. Running a program that tries to do everything is equivalent to having no brand.

I realize you may not see branding as part of a business plan but branding is what causes people to pay three times more for your service or product as they would for another. When someone thinks of you—you want them to know exactly what you do. When they think of your product—you want them to know exactly what that product will do for them. Therefore, branding needs to be a big part of your business plan because it powers the engine to your success.

MISSION, VISION, GOALS, AND OBJECTIVES

The next is *mission, vision, goals, and objectives*. I see so many executives struggle with their mission, vision, goals, and objectives. And quite honestly, this is not the place for me to explain how to develop these components—because that would amount to writing another book. However, your mission, vision, goals, and objectives are what provide a solid foundation so the big bad wolf can't huff and puff and blow your business down. And believe me, there is a big bad wolf out there, huffing and puffing on businesses as we speak. The dismal economy, the loss of grant funding, a decrease in program enrollment, and even the weather can devastate youth-serving programs. If you have a child care center, after-school program, or other direct care program a huge snow blizzard in your town could mean no money coming in—but you still have to pay rent. My point is that problems will come and you need to be properly prepared with a mission, vision, goals, and objectives that are strong enough to withstand the tests.

COMPANY NAME

The fourth area you can use to brand your business is your *company name, tagline, and logo.* Notice that I have included these in the latter part of branding your business—but many people make the mistake of doing this first. I recommend creating these last and if at all possible, after you get a firm grasp on the next pillar which is Clarity. You really cannot create a true brand if you don't have clarity—which I will talk about in the next chapter. For now, I encourage you to think about the name, tagline, and logo you've chosen because they are important. Be honest with yourself. Step back and look at them with fresh eyes. If you can't be objective because you are too attached—then ask a few people that don't know you. If as you go through the 6 Pillars, you realize you have not created the brand you desire to have—it's not too late to change, revise, or renovate. Actually, I recommend you take a hard look at your brand at least every couple of years. Branding is a journey, not a destination. Don't ever feel your brand is done. It's not. You will arrive—but then as your business grows and you learn more about your customers—your brand will also grow.

WHY SHOULD I CARE ABOUT MY BRAND?

Now that you have a better understanding of what branding is and is not, here are five reasons you should care. The first reason is because *a good brand will increase your credibility.* Professionally designed branding will give your business a consistent and cohesive image. I know it's tempting to make flyers on your computer and print them yourself but high quality materials will give your prospective customers the impression that your program is respectable, established, and professional. Potential customers will be much more likely to do business with *you* as opposed to a youth-serving organization, business, or program in your community that did not spend the money to brand professionally. That does not mean it has to be very expensive.

The second reason *you should care is because branding makes your business more memorable.* As a general rule, human beings remember far more of what they see than what they're told. Having a consistent image can make your brand more memorable. That's where a professional can create a graphic design that will keep your business in the forefront of your existing and prospective customer's mind. When they're looking for the products or services you offer—you want to come to their mind immediately. How many times have you needed to buy something and you couldn't remember the name of the company but you could clearly describe their logo or sing the jingle? You want your brand to leave the same impression.

It is important to create a brand that is identifiable. Consistency and image are both important but the most important thing—is that brand really isn't a "thing". Your brand is an experience. As you're thinking about how to brand your company, you need to remember to focus on the experience you want your customer to have and feel when they work with you. That's what people like. That's what people want. People fall in love with the feeling they get when they use your product or service—when they work with you or speak to you.

How many times have you traveled across town to eat at a specific restaurant, even though they don't have the best food or the best price? Now ask yourself why.

Lastly, keep in mind that as a youth-serving business you are in the unique position of needing to appeal to both the youth who use your service and the parents who pay the bill. A young person may love your program but if the parent does not like it, they are not going to pay. The parent may love your program but if their child complains every day the parent will likely take them out. That satisfaction dance can sometimes be very challenging but remain true to your brand plan. Do not change your branding to satisfy your customer. You need to brand based on your values—what you want to do—and what you are passionate about. This will attract your ideal customer—the ones that are the right fit for you.

Number three of why you should care about branding is *because it provides your customers with a sense of stability.* The number one reason large corporations' brand their business is to make sure they stand out from among all the other businesses in their industry. At the same time, they're creating a consistent and unique image for themselves. Most youth-serving organizations, businesses, or programs make the mistake of assuming that creating a brand is just for large companies or for-profit businesses. Nothing could be farther from the truth. If you don't get the branding right—everything else will fall apart and quickly. Honestly, branding can make or break your business success.

Let's face it. There's a youth-serving business popping up every day—especially if you're a child care center. Youth programs have a lot of competition—you have to make sure your customers know you will be there next week or they're not going to waste money or time doing business with you.

Number four of why you should care about branding is because *it differentiates your business from your competitors.* A well thought of brand will allow your program to easily highlight your core strength. If you don't know your core, you will not be able to build a brand (we will talk more about your core in the next chapter).

I see so many youth-serving programs offering way too many services. When you do that, the market isn't sure what you do well and I'm not sure you know what you do at all.

Here's the example I like to use for core strengths. You need brain surgery so you look for three doctors specializing in brain surgery. The first doctor says, *oh, yes. I can operate on your brain. I also do neck surgery and knee surgery.* The next doctor says, *oh, yes. I usually do brain surgery on children but I can operate on adults too.* You go to a third doctor who says, *absolutely. I do brain surgery and I specialize in females, between the age of 30 and 50.* Well, if you're a female age 42, you're thinking, *Bingo! I hit pay dirt now. This is my doctor. He knows his strength.*

Of course, I made that up but you have to identify your core so you can deliver a clear message. And once you are clear, you will build a brand that will skyrocket your business and your program. It's important to separate your program from your competitors in a way that your potential customers will easily be able to see and appreciate. A well-designed brand can place your program above your competitor—and if compared—you will win hands down.

In chapter 3 we are going to cover *marketing.* I bring that up now because when you pair your strong brand with an excellent marketing strategy—your competition will not win any day of the week against your business. If you live in an area with many of the same services you offer—creating a strong brand identity is crucial to developing a marketing plan that sets your program apart from the rest.

Reason number five for why you should care about branding is *because it will help you attract more clients.* A growing customer base is what all youth-serving organizations dream of. Well, all businesses dream of a growing customer base, right? But, the more kids you have come through your program—the more kids you help. So you definitely want to position yourself in a way that attracts more clients. You cannot help kids if you don't get them into your program. Having a polished and professional image will attract parents looking for a good program for their child. It doesn't matter what service you provide. If you are a youth-serving business in order to survive you need youth in your program.

There are many benefits to creating a brand identity but in order for a brand to be really effective—it has to get out there. You can have the best *brand* in the world, but if it's stuck in your computer or in your head—it's not going to help your program grow. Branding is going to come up again and again as we go through each pillar, especially *clarity, marketing, and visibility.* You cannot avoid branding so make it work for you instead of for your competitors.

I UNDERSTAND THE VALUE OF BRANDING. NOW WHAT?

Here are some strategies you can use right away to brand your business. Please be careful. If you have not identified or confirmed a solid brand—don't use these strategies until after you've gone through the Clarity chapter.

✦ **Company name.** Your company name is very important to your brand. Don't pick something crazy. Don't pick something hard to spell or hard to say. Also, make sure your company name can stand alone without the tagline or logo. I'll use my company as an example so that I'm not speaking ill of anyone else's name. *Empowering Youth for Success* is the name of my company. It is my brand. It stands alone. If you hear *Empowering Youth for Success*, you have some clue as to what I do. You might not know all the services I offer—but you know I'm doing something with youth that will help them succeed. Let's take a look at the association name—International Association of Youth Empowerment Programs—it's clear who the association was created to support.

✦ **Tagline.** If you are going to use a tagline it should be brief. It should be understandable and consistent with your business brand. It too needs the strength to stand alone. I see so many people choose weird business names and expect their tagline to explain the business. My tagline is, *Empowering Youth for Business, Financial, and Leadership Success.* That's it. If you see *empowering youth for business, financial, and leadership success*, you know exactly what I do. You don't need anything else. It's concise and to the point. Now what about the tagline for the association—"Youth-Serving Executives Building A Strong Foundation for Growth, Programming and Sustainability". That's clear too, right?

✦ **Logo.** If you're not a professional graphics designer, hire a professional to create your logo. Your logo should be easily understood and reflect your business brand. You want to use colors that don't lose their quality when transferred to marketing materials. Sometimes, businesses create logos that are so detailed that the image becomes distorted.

✦ **Domain name.** You want your brand in front of your ideal customer whenever possible, so your website domain name should be the same as your brand name. That's why my website is also www.EmpoweringYouthforSuccess.com. You want a web addresses that is easy and try to always end your domain name with ".com"—so your prospects have no trouble finding your site. Your web address is not the place to be cute. Be creative with your message but not in the spelling—because guess what? A misspelled web address takes them to someone else's business. Also, keep in mind that long domain names can be difficult for your customers to spell and remember. My domain name is longer than it should be but sometimes the perfect brand outweighs best practice.

✦ **Good customer support.** Word of mouth is the best branding you can get. On the other hand, it can be the worst branding too. People will always be impressed by good customer service. And they'll tell all their friends and family members about your business. Remember, your success is in the details.

✦ **Email branding.** Make use of the space at the end of your emails to brand your business. If you do an online newsletter, make sure you put your branding in the subject line to let your subscribers know the email is from your company. You can also put your logo in the body of your email messages. The more people see your name or logo the more your brand becomes ingrained in their mind.

✦ **Product.** Your youth-serving program should have a unique signature product, program, or service so when your ideal client has a need they will immediately think of your business. By the end of this book you will realize that my signature program for youth-serving executives is 6 Pillars to Success.

You have now read the first pillar, Branding. I encourage you to go through each of the four general brand areas and use your notebook to brain storm ideas for your youth-serving program. I look forward to sharing chapter two. Won't you join me?

3

Success Pillar #2: Clarity

n the previous section, we focused on Pillar One, Branding. We discussed the importance of proper branding for your success. Now that you have worked through pillar one let's move on to pillar two, Clarity. If Branding is the queen to your success, then Clarity can be considered the king. You will have difficulty moving forward with your program until you have these two pillars firmly under your belt.

Let's talk about Clarity.

Simply stated, clarity can be defined as knowing what you want and then designing your ideal business. It means finding your focus instead of wandering around in the wilderness serving in areas that do not relate to what you intended your business to be. This is one of the most difficult pillars for any business—nonprofit, for profit, entrepreneur, small business, or brick and mortar. Once you have clarity about your program— you can make it happen a whole lot faster. There are four things I want to cover in chapter two as it relates to clarity. To achieve true clarity in any business you need to have a core plan, recognize your power performance, be able to identify your target market, and describe your ideal client.

Let's discuss those one at a time.

CORE PLAN

The first thing I want to cover is a Core Plan. Exactly what do I mean when I say core plan? To determine your core plan—you must ask yourself "What do I want the focus of my program to be?" It is really easy to get caught up in offering services simply because you know how or the services are requested. And, since you are capable of doing the service, you do it. On another note, you may offer services because you need the money or because it's something you enjoy. This book is called *Passion Won't Pay The Bills*, so I truly understand your need for paying customers to sustain your business. But I caution you to be careful—you may look up one day to find a program you do not like. It is essential that you know your core in order to achieve clarity.

So, what is your core?

I will again use my business as an example. The focus for Empowering Youth for Success is exactly what the title says – to empower youth for success. But that could be success in sports, success on the SAT—success in what? I determined my core to be financial, business and leadership success. Is your core something easy to recognize or are you operating more like a starfish or octopus serving in a bunch of different areas but not actually connecting to your strength? Clarity is king. It is your leader. But it's up to you. It is not up to your client or what people say about your program.

The following example proves how easy it can be to get away from your core or better yet, not have one at all. I like to use child care examples because I owned child care centers for so long. When you open a child care center you often have a target age in mind. But, because you are trying to get the business going—you stray away from that target age and begin accepting children you really do not want to take. You may end up taking a school age child simply because the preschool sibling is in the program. Tutoring is another example. A business begins with tutoring as a core but then a parent needs transportation. Before long, the business core is out the window and the program is now offering tutoring and transportation. The same can be said for the tutoring subjects. You may set out to only tutor math—but at the request of the parent—additional subjects are added. Suddenly, you find yourself tutoring a subject you do not have expertise in and your tutoring business is hardly recognizable because you have strayed away from your core.

So, that's number one. To achieve clarity you must have a core plan.

- What do you want the focus of your business to be? *Word of mouth is the fastest way to grow a business.*

- If someone is going to talk about your business what do you want them to say?

- What is it that you want to be known for?

- If the city put up a billboard about your services—what exactly do you want those passing by to learn about your business?

- What would you want them to drive away knowing—without a shadow of a doubt—about your program and your core?

POWER PERFORMANCE

The second area I want to discuss is what I call power performance. Your power performance is defined by what you do really well. When you start stepping into areas that are not within your skills and abilities—many things can happen and they all result in not having customers and clients. One, your business or program fails to grow because you begin watering down your message. How? You begin offering services you don't do well and clients begin giving negative reviews about your program. Be cautious about offering services just because you can. Two, if you offer services outside the realm of your gifts and talents; you will have a difficult time branding your program. In fact you will create a conflicting brand. It happens to the best of us because branding is a process—as I mentioned in chapter two. It's the same thing with clarity. Don't be too hard on yourself if you're having difficulty getting the clarity and focus you need. It takes time, thought and research. The questions throughout this chapter should help you clear away some of the fog—then you can build your program on the strength and power of your core.

When I discussed branding, I talked about setting yourself apart. Your program needs to be different from your competition. What is it that makes a customer, client, or parent decide they're going to choose your program over one that is just like yours and only two blocks down the street? Always know that people have money and they will spend money when they feel it is worth the investment. In truth, it is rarely about the money. If that were the case many youth-serving programs would not exist because there are government agencies offering the same services for free. Why would parents pay for programs that cost money when they can get those same services for free? Your job is to position yourself to give prospective clients a reason to pay for your program.

Your place of power is one of the strengths you can use in your marketing and branding to set you apart. So again, using Empowering Youth for Success as an example, I certainly am one of the rare coaches who specialize in youth-serving programs. That's important and is probably one of the major factors that drew you to this book. There are a lot of other books out there that can teach you how to start a business, how to run a business, how to grow a business, how to sustain a business, how to brand, etc. But you and I know there is something totally different about a youth-serving program and the youth empowerment market. You'll quickly find in listening to other business coaches—the same general business principles—but the youth-serving market is extremely unique. The average business coach is never going to understand our market nuances unless they've been in the youth-serving business. That is one major thing that sets me apart from other business coaches. I use my place of power and strength to help youth-serving executives build a thriving heart-centered business.

What and where is your power?

You have to tap into your power and not be afraid to use it in your branding to promote your difference. Once you have established a core focus for your program—you must harness the power of what you do well. These are both essential in achieving clarity.

TARGET MARKET

A third important factor in achieving clarity is identifying your target market. When I work with youth-serving programs—in private or group coaching sessions—I often ask "Who is your target market?" Your target market is defined by who needs your services—which right away presents a dilemma for youth-serving executives because your market is two-fold. Be careful not to get hung up on the word "need". From a marketing perspective—keep in mind that people don't buy what they need—they buy what they want. Unfortunately, parents may not want your program or service until they reach an unbearable level of pain. Their child could be in deep trouble or facing grade level failure before a parent reaches the point of paying for your services. So back to "Who needs your program?" As I mentioned earlier, you must appeal to both the youth who will be the ultimate consumer and the parents who pay the bill. If the youth are not happy, parents will not be willing to pay for the service or you may have a child who is totally sold on your program and the parent isn't. You may sometimes feel like you're caught between a rock and a hard place but when you think about your target market you must consider the wants of the youth and the parent.

Now that you are reminded of the "satisfaction dance" I can move deeper into identifying your target market. When I ask youth-serving executives to name their target market, many respond "youth," "parents" or "both"; however, in order to have an effective marketing plan, you must be clear on your target market. Even though you must consider the wants of the youth—the "parent" is your target market because they have the money to pay for the service. But with so many parents in the world you still need to be more specific. You will never run out of parents so don't be afraid to narrow your target market. Create a profile of the parent who needs your program or service by asking questions like:

✦ What type of parents are you targeting?

✦ Are they parents that live in your town?

✦ Are they military parents?

✦ Do they live within 5 blocks of your business?

✦ Are they self-employed?

My suggestion is to start thinking more narrow than just "parents." By being very clear, the type of parent you are targeting will recognize themselves in your advertising. Choosing your target market and narrowly defining the group is critical for clarity.

IDEAL CLIENT PROFILE

After choosing your target market, you must determine your ideal client. This is not to be confused with your target market. Remember, target market is who needs your service. Identifying a target market means you have narrowed down who would want and be willing to pay for your service, where they live, are they black—are they blue, do they have husbands, etc. This helps determine who to target. However, it does not identify your ideal client. Your ideal client is the person *you want* to work with. You will not get excited about working with everyone in your target market. It is important to understand— that everyone is not your ideal client. This person may need your service, they may have the money to pay for your service, they may want your service—but they may pluck your last nerve. They are not your ideal client, and that's okay. This is your program—this is your business, and even though you're in it to serve youth—it doesn't mean you should be unhappy doing it.

You have the authority to choose the people who enter your program. In reality you will not enjoy working with all kids or parents. Your goal is to fill your program with clients you enjoy.

✦ What is your ideal client like?

✦ What do they do and how do they act?

Begin to formulate a list describing your ideal client. Begin by saying "I prefer to work with parents who _____. I prefer to work with youth who _____." Personally, I prefer to work with people who are action takers because I'm an action taker. Figure out what resonates with you as a person and what you want for your business. I encourage you to start writing down what your ideal client looks like—what they do—what they say—how they dress. One of the first things you'll probably say is "Your ideal client has the money to pay and pay on time." Delinquent payments are a big issue for a lot of youth-serving programs. The parents either don't pay or they pay late. And, many parents are not willing to pay what you are worth. Difficulties are sure to arise but you have to resist the urge to allow the parents' financial problems to put a strain on your bank account.

Let me give you a quick suggestion for parents who have difficulty paying for your services—offer them a scholarship. When I had my child care center, I created a scholarship be-cause at some point we all have problems. The scholarship was twice a year—it ran from January to June and July to December. A parent having financial problems could apply for the schol-arship and their child would be allowed to attend my child-care center for that six month period without paying tuition—to give the parent a chance to recover. I was being supportive and helpful, without sending my business to the poor house. I created an application form with a required essay question and when a parent came to me with a need I said—"I'm really sorry to hear that you're going through hard times—let me give you an application for our scholarship program". Interestingly enough, in 10 years I only had two parents use the scholarship. When people run into a financial bind, their first reaction is to see who they can pay late. Your program quickly comes to mind because it seems easier than trying to negotiate the electric bill or car payment. However, when you put parents in a situation where they have to do something—it encourages them to find a way to solve their problem and still pay you. You can tweak the scholarship concept to offer a specific number of slots in your tutoring program at a reduced rate. It doesn't matter how you do it but create a system you are comfortable with—that is financially feasible and stick to it. You deserve to get paid for your services and your ideal client will respect that.

Before we move on, let's review some basics. First, I want you to think about your gift to the world? What is it that you do better than anyone else—what is your purpose—what is the reason your program exists? There is something so awesome about finally getting to the place where you are living your purpose and you wake up every day knowing you're doing exactly what you were put on this earth to do. That's how I feel every day, no matter how much I have to do that day or how tired I may be—I just feel great when I wake up in the morning because I'm living my purpose.

Here are some questions to help you reach clarity:

✦ What causes people to seek you out regularly?

✦ For what do you want to become known as the go to person?

✦ What is it you want your program to be known for?

✦ If somebody needs _____ you want other people to say, "You know what? You need to go to Linette Daniels if you are trying to grow or sustain your youth-serving program."

✦ What activity engages you so fully that time slips away before you notice?

Those are some of the questions I want you to ask as it relates to coming up with your core plan and your power performance. Don't worry about having too many answers, you may have three things that are your gift to the world, but you'll start out focusing on one.

Here are some more questions:

✦ Who needs your gift?

✦ Out of all the people in the whole world, what are the qualities of the people who need your gift?

✦ What gender are they?

✦ Where do they live?

✦ How old are they?

✦ How much money do they make?

✦ What do they do for a living?

You want to use as many adjectives as you can think of to describe these people. Literally give your ideal client a name and turn them into a person you can visualize. This will be golden when we work on marketing, visibility and programming.

Once you've figured out what you do and who needs what you do—your next step is to determine the specific qualities of your ideal client.

+ What do you ideal clients think about?

+ What are their beliefs?

+ What values do they hold dear?

+ What industries are they in?

+ What are their traits and qualities?

+ What is it that you enjoy about working with them or being around them?

+ Are there issues that need to be addressed before someone is ready to work with you?

FREEZE

In my business the 6 Pillars to Success is a required prerequisite because they set the foundation for your program. My ideal client has the option of completing the home study version prior to working with me or completing the pillars in one of my group or private coaching programs. You may have something foundational in your program. If you do tutoring or something related to better grades in school—you may have an entrance test they have to take. You may require parents to volunteer 10 hours a month in order for their child to participate in your program. In my eyes, the 6 Pillars are the foundation to success for youth-serving programs. What do you consider the foundation of success for your clients?

Now that you have your target market narrowed down, you must determine if it is a viable market.

+ Is it worth your time, energy, effort and money to focus on that group of people?

+ Is there a list of them?

+ Is there a civic group or a professional association or support group for them?

+ Is there some place they all hang-out together?

It is always better to market to a group of your ideal clients than trying to market one to one.

+ Where do they hang out?

+ Can you find them in discussion groups, blogs, forums, networking sites?

+ Can you open the Yellow Pages and find them?

+ What type of magazine do they like to read?

+ Where do they network?

+ Are they part of a particular industry or profession?

Maybe your youth program offers a service that is ideal for parents working in real estate. Another good way to find your ideal client is by asking who they do business with. Think of other businesses that have the same ideal client and see if you can collaborate to reach that ideal client.

PILLAR STUDY

I have a client who is a college recruiter—he helps athletes get into college on an athletic scholarship. During a recent conversation I helped him identify collaborative opportunities. For him a sporting goods store, like Dick's Sporting Goods is ideal. Dick's sells basketballs, shoes, sporting gear etc. so my client's target market would be the same as Dick's target market. I helped my client create a marketing plan that would involve collaborating with the sporting goods store— to connect with and learn more about his prospects from a store that is already spending money to reach that market.

While this may seem simple—you may discover what you thought was a feasible target market is not. If you're unable to find groups of people that fit your description—go back to the drawing board until you come up with a target market you can reach, touch and communicate with—online and/or offline. If you can't find them, you have no way of marketing to them. You have no way of drawing them in. If you don't know who they are, you have no way of reaching them. If you don't know your power—you won't know what to tell them if you reach them. If you don't know your core—you don't have anything to offer when you reach them. Going back to the drawing board to find a worthy market for your services may be a lot of work but it is part of obtaining the clarity you need to be successful. Can you see how all of these aspects work together? Knowing your core—your power—and who your target and ideal clients are is crucial for obtaining clarity.

Now what?

You're going to determine why a customer would want to buy your products and services—you're going to identify the products and services you are good at—you're going to determine your target market and your ideal client—and then you're going to determine if that is a viable market and if it's feasible for you to move forward with the market you are considering.

Achieving clarity can be a daunting endeavor but having branding and clarity down to a science will be the fastest path to success. The program executives who fully understand Pillar #1 and Pillar #2 will save time, energy, effort and money implementing the strategies in the remaining chapters.

PILLAR CHALLENGE

Take your ideal client description and go through your database of past and current parents—identifying those who meet your criteria and survey them. You can do a paper survey, an online survey or you can simply do 15 minute interviews over the telephone. Regardless of the tool you use to assess your market—it is important to ask questions that allow you to learn more about your ideal client. Conducting this survey will help you really hone and learn more about the people who are drawn to your program. (You are welcome to use or tweak one of the surveys I use. Visit **www.iayep.com/samplesurvey**) It is also beneficial to choose a parent you enjoy working with and make a list of everything you love about them. Then select a parent you don't like working with and write a list of everything about them that drives you bananas. I want you to do the same thing for a child. Think of the student in your program that you just love and then think of the child you were happy went on vacation. This exercise can greatly assist in building the profile for your ideal client but only if you are honest.

4

Success Pillar #3: Marketing

Perhaps the most highly anticipated session I do with clients who take part in my programs is the marketing pillar. I'm sure the same can be said for you. You've probably been looking forward to this chapter all along. Remember, it is very important that you have strong pillars one and two before you begin work on the marketing pillar. But, here we find ourselves.

Identifying your target market and ideal client is hard work. After all these years, I still step back and re-evaluate my market and my ideal client. It is essential for you to reevaluate your ideal client—your target market—and your branding too.

If you are basically an offline program, this chapter is going to be very important to your success. You will need to leave your comfort zone to develop an online presence for your program. Even if everything you do is in your community, Ms Jones—who lives down the street from your business—still wants to research your program before she calls or comes to visit. That means your prospective clients will look online for information about your programs and services. Unfortunately—and it may not be fair to offline programs—in this day and time when people go to the internet and they don't find a website—they feel like you are not a real business. By not having an online presence, you are losing countless numbers of potential customers. If they can't find you—chances are they won't buy from you. Having a website says you are a serious player in the market. To some, developing a website may be very scary. Others may have a website but aren't using it to its fullest potential. Either way, you are missing a great opportunity.

The four marketing areas that are really important for you to focus on—all stem from branding and clarity. The first one—which we have briefly discussed above—is the online presence. Included in this chapter is also information on listing building, an autoresponder, and blogging. All four of these tools are essential to successful marketing; however, the majority of this chapter will focus on your website because it is the launching pad for the other three.

Before I begin, keep in mind that offline businesses need to have an online presence just as much as online businesses need to get out into the community. It is going to take a combination of marketing and visibility to create a successful online-offline presence. I will talk about visibility in chapter five.

HAVING AN ONLINE PRESENCE

Having a website is very important to your business and marketing your program or service. If the website is not done, or if it is not done well, you are not *marketing* to your fullest potential. This could be causing your business to suffer or even fail. Before I begin discussing marketing in further detail, let me tell you five things that may be causing your ideal client not to buy from you or enroll in your program. Many of the five are related to having an online presence and proper marketing strategies. As I go over them—ask yourself if you fall into one or more of the categories.

The number one reason your ideal client may not be using your services is that your *ideal client can't find you.* You don't have a website. You don't have a blog. You think social media is a waste of time or you're not sure how to use it to grow your program. Whatever your reason—you have chosen not to use the benefits of social media to drive people to your business and this could be greatly affecting your marketing practices and actual buyer potential.

It is important to make yourself available to your ideal clients.

- Are you sharing your knowledge and giving potential clients a way to get to know more about you and your area of expertise?

- Are you hanging out where your ideal clients hang out?

- Are you developing relationships and asking for referrals?

Teaching your clients how to bring you more clients is important in marketing. Make it easy for them to send you more clients by asking them to refer you to friends and family.

Sharing your knowledge and giving your potential clients the opportunity to get to know more about you and your expertise can be difficult and time consuming. This is especially true if you rely on networking events, meetings and committees to get the word out about your program. The online community and social media specifically—provide a fast track easy way to market that does not happen in the offline world. This is why it is essential that you have a website to market your business. Your website allows you to display your expertise, to show off your program, and share your special events without having to physically be everywhere at once. Developing a strong website needs to be your primary online focus.

The second thing that may be causing your ideal client not to buy from you is *your ideal clients don't know they are your ideal client.* Are you clear about your target market and the kind of people you want to work with? If you aren't, how can you expect your prospects to know they're your ideal client? Will you work with just anybody? No, any parent that's breathing and has money in the bank is not your ideal client. Once you get crystal clear on your ideal client and properly market to them—you'll be like a magnet. Your ideal client will start to be drawn to you because you're sending the right signal. Get clear and stop trying to be everything to everyone. Clarity will make it much easier for prospects to say *yes*—and for you to say *yes.* Someone contacting you about your program or service is just as much an interview of them—as it is of you. Saying no to the clients who are not ideal makes room for the ones who are. Don't be afraid to turn down business from people who do not fit your ideal client description. Doing so ensures that you stay true to your brand and are not sacrificing your vision for monetary gain.

The third reason is that *you're making it difficult for your ideal client to do business with you.* Now why would you do something like that, when you need the money, right? But there are lots of ways you do just that. It's not your fault—you don't know what you don't know. First I want to talk about your business card. I don't know how many times I've met someone—asked for a business card—and when they can't find one they say *oh, I must have just given out my last card.* Check your supply before you leave home—you never know where you will meet your next customer. It also drives me bananas when someone gives me a card with things crossed off and new information written on top. That's not professional. That is not good for business. When you do little things like that—you are branding your company. Your business card speaks volumes about the quality of your program. If you can't take time or a few dollars to get new cards—your prospective clients may not take you seriously, number one—and this leads to number two, the increased likelihood that your customers won't adhere to your program rules. It sounds silly but this is what can happen all because of a business card—and by golly please don't pull out the business card and scribble through information right in front of them. That's really horrible. Your business card should provide accurate information about your service and more importantly— how you can be contacted. Potential clients want to know your phone number and they definitely want your email and web address. Get a nice professionally tailored business card that has your information readily available for potential and current clients alike.

Here are a few more tips for allowing your customers to do business with you more easily. Pay close attention to the email address you put on your card. If you have a Yahoo or Hotmail address consider making a change. These email addresses are unprofessional and can hurt your business image. They say to your prospective client that you are not a real business. For example, my email address is linette@empoweringyouthforsuccess.com or linette@iayep.com. A website email address is what people expect from a business. If you are going to totally defy getting a website—the one free email that people still find acceptable in the business world—is Gmail—probably because it's owned by Google. You can go to **www.gmail.com** and open an account.

I also recommend you not use a free website. While some free websites look good and can effectively market your program—they are not acceptable in the business world. I know money is tight but when someone goes to your website and it says *click here to get your free website too*—it places your program in a different category. It knocks you down to a level that harshly affects your branding. Pay the extra money to get a website and allow other players in the market to know you are serious about the brand you are building. It's not about the money—it the value you display to your prospective client. You also want to make sure the information on your website is accurate. If your website is missing your phone number, mailing address, and email address your clients will not be able to contact you. If your clients have a difficult time locating things on your website—you are losing potential business. If your website uses a lot of program specific jargon you are making it difficult for your ideal client to do business with you. You may have gone to school years ago for marketing but the internet has very different marketing rules from what you learned in school. It's a totally different world—the technology has created expectations you weren't prepared for.

It is also important to look for every opportunity to market your program or services. The smallest marketing opportunities can make it easier for your potential client to do business with you. An example is the recorded greeting on your voicemail. My voicemail might say, *"Hi, this is Linette founder of the International Association of Youth Empowerment Programs. I'm sorry I've missed your call. Please leave a message. And in the meantime, you might want to know about the upcoming class I have for youth-serving executives. The class starts on March 1ˢᵗ. To learn more about increasing your program success visit us at www.iayep.com. Thank you."* Take every opportunity to showcase your brand. Before I move on I will be remiss if I don't also address your home and cell phone. You never know when someone will get a hold of your home or cell phone number so even though you don't use it for business—please make sure the greeting and music is appropriate. I can't count the number of times I called to offer someone a job and changed my mind after I heard their voice-mail.

The number four reason your ideal client may not be doing business with you is because *you're not demonstrating the value of your services.* You must demonstrate why your client should choose your service instead of going down the street to a program that's cheaper or the agency that is free. You need to always remember in everything you do—at all times, in all places, and in all ways—your potential client and your current client are always thinking, WIIFM. What's in it for me? This is not about you. It's about your client. Understanding this is critical to getting your ideal client to choose your services. Does your brochure list a bunch of services or does it demonstrate how your program can solve your market's problem? Does your website look like an online catalog or does it offer a way to erase your market's pain? You need to promote the problems your program solves or what pain you eliminate for potential clients.

The fifth reason is *you're making it difficult for your ideal client to invest in your program or services.* You may provide a SAT prep service that parents need, want, and are willing to pay for but maybe they are not sure about you. Before they invest in your program they want to feel comfortable that you can really help their child pass the SAT. Do you have an introductory offer to your program or services that make prospects want to invest with you? Do you have something that allows the parent to get to know you or experience your program? You can get a parent to choose your program over a free program any day of the week—but it's about building the relationship and the experience. The key to your success is to offer an experience. Potential clients want a taste of your business. Consider offering a free trial or allowing the client to sit in on a session or attending a day at no charge. Also determine whether it is important for the parent to take part in the experience with their child.

PILLAR STUDY

My daughter was a competition cheerleader for years. I spent about $15,000 a year for her to cheer and that did not include all the travel expenses—so when it came time to try out for a new cheerleading squad—it was a big decision. If I'm going to spend that kind of money—I want to make sure it's a good gym and they treat her well. Most of the cheer programs offered a complimentary session so she could practice with the squad and get to know the coaches—before I made my decision and signed a yearlong contract. This opportunity proved vital because I was very unhappy with the gym *we thought* was our first choice.

PILLAR STUDY

I was choosing between two different dentists. They had the same prices—located the same distance from my house—offered the same services—and same yucky gum cleaner, but the dentist I chose offered an experience. When I walked in the door they offered me a cappuccino. They literally have a menu with juice, coffee, hot chocolate, latte, bottled water etc. I don't drink coffee and I don't like chocolate but I was very impressed by the menu and the offer. And guess what—they use real teacups and saucers. And guess what else—it's free. So which dentist do you think I chose? I've been there for four years now and have not taken them up on an offer yet (of course my kids have). But they sold me on the experience.

PILLAR CHALLENGE

Determine three ways you can create an experience for your prospective and current clients.

Your payment methods may also make it difficult for your ideal client to invest in your program. Are payment plans available for your higher priced services? For some clients a payment plan can make or break the deal. Adding a service charge for payment plans is fine. This way, both you and the client win.

I encourage you to take credit cards. If you are not taking credit cards—you are letting money walk out the door. A lot of people have turned to using credit/debit cards instead of cash or checks. The key is making it easy for your client to invest in your program. Making it difficult to pay for your services is a marketing mishap that drives business away. The forms of payment you accept can be damaging the success of your business—at the very least consider using PayPal.

The sixth and final reason your ideal client may not be buying from you is a *lack of established credibility in the mind of your prospects.* Make sure you have an About Me page on your website. Your visitors want to know who you are and what makes you the person that can solve their problem or fill their need. By law, you are required to have your address on your website but it can be a Post Office Box. Absolutely do not use your home address. Your picture, an address and a phone number on your website will help establish credibility. Please take a professional picture. A picture of you sitting at your kitchen table or riding in your car is not appropriate for business. If you do workshops or keynotes—add a picture of you speaking. Pictures of you interacting with kids are also great. Most importantly—visitors want to see your face—your eyes and your smile. This is critical. No one wants to do business with somebody who looks like they ate lemons for breakfast. Visitors get to know you through your picture so make it count. Look directly into the camera— not down, not over, not off to the side. Look directly into the camera—and smile.

Now that I have covered the six reasons your ideal client may not be using your services—let's focus again on your online presence or website. No matter how great your website or how much time or money you put into creating a website—if it's aimed at the wrong people—it's not going to be successful. This is where knowing your target market comes into play. If you know your target market—you will be able to speak their language. What you say to a single parent is different from the words you would use with a married couple. The goal of your website is to make your ideal client say—"hey, that's me". You will not only offer products and services they want, but you'll be able to—write and use words, stories, language, and even colors—that will attractive them.

Make your website useful by making it easy for visitors to determine if your products or services are right for them. Answer your potential customers' questions before their mind asks for you. Visitors may really like your website, your prices and your program—but don't expect them to call or email with questions. They may write your telephone number down and plan to call—but it will only take seconds before something in their life takes priority and they forget all about you. Even when it is important to them—they may forget. Put yourself in the customer's shoes and provide everything that they need or want to make an informed decision about your program. If you know enough about your target market and your ideal clients— this task will be a lot easier. This is where the survey I spoke of earlier will really help—as will frequenting the forums and blogs where your target market hangs out. Going to forums and blogs is a great way to find out what parents need—what they want—and what they're frustrated by so you can use their language to offer services that solve the problems they expressed.

PILLAR STUDY

When you hear parents complain about youth programs that close at 5 o'clock and you have a program that's open till 5:30—the words on your website and brochure should highlight your understanding of their problem and the solution you offer. Example: *I know how difficult it is when you don't get off work until five or five thirty and so many youth programs close at five o'clock.* Use *their* words in your marketing materials, on the telephone, and in person. Mirror what your prospective and current clients are experiencing or feeling. Unless you know your target market, you will be unable to speak in their voice. As you get to know your customers more and more—you will be able to tweak your website to cater to them.

FREEZE

Speaking in your ideal client's voice is critical—and often times their words will not be grammatically correct—but that's okay in marketing.

Answer your prospect's questions and consider doing it in list format. A FAQ page on your website can be very beneficial for visitors. You could also allow visitors to ask questions directly on your website. The answer can come in the form of a blog post, which we will discuss later in this chapter. Think about it this way—a question is actually a doubt. If they have too many doubts—they're not going to buy. If you answer all the questions you can think of, you've eliminated a host of obstacles to them signing up for your program. Use your web-site as an opportunity to do more than sell your product. Use it as an opportunity to build the relationship. The relationship is what will cause a parent to walk past a free program—straight into your doors.

You need to step back quarterly or at least annually to evalu-ate your website with fresh eyes. What worked with your target market before may not work later. These same concepts regard-ing your website also apply to using brochures and flyers to ef-fectively market your business. In fact—you should have goals for your website and other marketing materials. Once you have goals and take the actions needed to draw your ideal client to your website—you want a way to keep track of who is visiting. You also want a way to get your visitors contact information when they come to your website. It doesn't help for people to visit your website if you don't know they've been there—and you don't have a way to keep in touch with them. This is the next marketing tool I am going to teach. By the way—it is also a good idea to make information available to people who visit your building after hours and even better if you have a way to track who has been there.

LIST BUILDING

List building means you are growing a list of prospective clients—customers—or parents. In order to grow the list you need a system on your website that keeps track of visitor names and email addresses. Look at every single visit to your website as potential business. Statistically speaking—it takes at least 7 to 10 contacts before a prospect makes the decision to buy. That means they are not likely to buy the first time they come to your website. In fact, they may never come to your website again—

so make every effort to get them on your mailing list—at the first visit.

It will be difficult to get visitors to leave their information on your site if there's nothing in it for them. Remember WIIFM? You need to give them something for free in exchange for their contact information. We call this an ethical bribe or irresistible gift. It may be a free day or week in your program. It could be a coupon for your services. The only rule is—it has to be something they perceive as valuable in order to get their information.

AUTORESPONDERS

List-building and autoresponders work together to form a very powerful marketing strategy. An autoresponder provides your website with an "opt-in" box that collects and manages the names and email addresses of your website visitors. Outlook, Yahoo, Hotmail, and Gmail are not autoresponders. With an autoresponder service, all of the email addresses are collected electronically. Then let's say, you have 1,000 names and email addresses in the autoresponder and you want to send an email about a special next week on your tutoring service. You can type one email—push send and it will automatically go to all 1,000 people without you having to do anything else. That's the value of an autoresponder service. There are lots of other ways an autoresponder can help grow your business but for now an autoresponder will save you time—get your marketing message out to a small or large audience—and allow you to continue marketing to potential clients long after they leave your website.

Autoresponders are also a good way to bring new traffic to your website. Let's use the example of giving a free week as an incentive. While talking to a potential client about your program—you can tell them that all the information you are explaining is available free on your website. You might say something like—*"Let me tell you how your child can come here for a week for free so you can try it out. All you have to do is go to my website and you'll see where you can get a free week trial just for putting your name and email address in the box. That's it. The coupon for your free week will be sent to your email address. Once you have the coupon, just call and set up your free week."* Parents are always willing to take what they can get for free. Chances are—they will go to your website and complete the opt-in box—which in turn puts them on your list of prospects. Sure, you could hand them a coupon but when they leave your building—that's it—they are gone. Being able to market to them again and again through the autoresponder will reap rewards later down the road. If it is going to take seven to ten contacts before they're ready to make a buying decision—an autoresponder is the best way to do it. Once they are on your list, continue to offer great tips and resources and turning them into clients will be a cinch.

FREEZE

Your building should have a sign-in sheet to collect the names, addresses and emails of onsite visitors as well.

Your opt-in box is another area of your website that must be monitored. If you have the opt-in box on your website and no one is signing up—there could be a couple of reasons. One, people aren't going to your website or two; your free offer is not appealing to them. Don't be put off by having to monitor your website. It's a process just like tracking the return on investment for your offline marketing expenses. But the more you know about your ideal client—the less time, money, effort, and energy—you will waste on marketing that doesn't work.

You can either invest time researching or waste time creating programs and services your market does not want. I've done it both ways. And trust me—it's a lot less aggravating if you do the research upfront.

BLOGGING

Blogging is a difficult concept for some people while easy for others. You can turn blogging into a major marketing tool that works wonders for your program growth. Blogging is basically just writing. It is a miniature form of an article or story that gives tips, tools, or resources to your readers. There are many different ways to blog. Look at websites like mine (**www.IAYEP.com**) to get ideas on blogging. You will find articles about marketing your program, increasing enrollment, empowering youth, etc. A variety of topics geared towards helping you—*my ideal client.*

Blogging provides substance to a website. When blogging is available—the website is offering more to your visitor than a "buy" button. Blogging can be an important part of branding because it helps you build a reputation—establish a relationship—and position your program as the go to place for the service your offer.

If you use blogging as a marketing tool on your website—be consistent with posting information. Are you going to blog 2 days a week? If so, which two days? If you decide to only blog once a week—that's fine but consistency is a must. If I come to your website on Monday because Monday is when you blogged last week and I don't see a new article I may come back on Tuesday—but if it's still not there I am not likely to return. Your visitors are not going to chase you, no matter how great the information you provide. Your blogging schedule can be whatever you want—just decide and stick to it. The more you blog—the better result you will get from this marketing tool. You can hire someone to blog for you to ensure consistently—you can also write blog posts ahead of time and schedule them to post automatically to your website on a specific date and time. Remember I said earlier—you have to make it easy for your customer to give you money. Blogging is a very helpful tool for success—whether you are an online or offline program.

You may be a bit overwhelmed at the end of this marketing chapter so let me recap.

A good website will not be born over night. It takes time or money. In many cases it takes both. Your website needs credibility. You need to provide the name of your business, a physical address, an email address, and a phone number where you can be reached. Another way to get credibility is to put your photo on the website for your potential clients to connect a face with your business. This allows potential clients to see a real person. A confused mind does not buy so try to make your site user-friendly and easy to navigate. When you design the website put yourself in a buyer's shoes. Buyers do not want to be overwhelmed. Make things easy to find with tab titles that make sense. Do not just tell clients about the services you offer—but explain how your program will help them. In most cases, price is especially important to include on your website. This is probably the number one thing potential clients look for when they visit. Be sure to explain how to go about using your services or enrolling in your program. You may even allow online enrollment as an incentive to save time and money. Potential clients who visit your website want tips, tools, help, and resources. Most importantly—they want it for free.

Don't fret, I can show you exactly how to get it all done. You can see through my stressing of the online presence how important it is to market your business properly. You need a strong online presence in order to build and grow your program. To do this you need a website, a list building strategy, an autoresponder service, and a blogging schedule. Together—these four marketing tools can skyrocket your program to places you never thought possible. Once you have your Branding – "who are you?", and your Clarity – "who is your client?" you can focus on Marketing—"how will you grow?"

5

Success Pillar #4: Visibility

Welcome to Pillar #4. I am so proud of you for being willing to get out-of-the-box and look at program building in different ways. I hope you are starting to see the puzzle pieces come together. You cannot expect your business to be successful from just one pillar. You need all six pieces of the puzzle. Furthermore—each pillar has to be strong in order to support your program growth.

In this chapter I am going to talk about visibility. When I say the word visibility, I am talking about how you are connecting with your target market. Do not get Visibility confused with Marketing. While the two may seem the same—they are very different pillars in creating a successful business. Marketing is putting yourself out there and making your information available to potential clients. Visibility can be defined by actually building relationships with those potential clients. How you connect to your target market makes all the difference to your program success.

There are a number of Visibility tools I could give you—however—through this chapter I am going to address the four strategies I feel are most important at this point in the business world—both online and offline. Before I share the cornerstones of visibility—it is pertinent for you to embrace the "bottom line" for this pillar—to be successful in your business and to achieve maximum visibility you must have what the industry refers to as "Know, Like, and Trust". When people come into your brick and mortar building—they are not going to just walk in the door—hand you money and leave. You build a rapport with them from the time you say—"Hello, welcome to the International Association of Youth Empowerment Programs, how can I help you?" The same is true when prospects call on the telephone. You must build a relationship.

In the offline world—your customers can see you. They can shake your hand. They can hear your tone of voice. They can feel your aura. But in the online world—making that connection takes more effort. You have to be consistent and visible in a variety of ways for people to know you.

Remember, until they know you—they can't like you—and they can't trust you. And until they "Know, Like, and Trust" you—they're not going to buy—they're not going to enroll their child. This means *really* connecting with your potential clients in an authentic way. They may talk about you in the community. And they may read about you online. But until you build the "Know, Like, and Trust" factor—watching is as far as the relationship will go. Whether your business is brick and mortar or online—building rapport with existing and potential clients will drive your business to the next level of success. In chapter 4 we discussed the importance of having a picture on your website. This rings true with visibility as well. If your prospects need to "know, like, and trust" you before they buy from you—they need a face to go with your business. The four strategies of Visibility: live events, creating video, article marketing, and using social media. We will explore each of these individually.

LIVE EVENTS

Live Events can be an important and useful tool for building visibility in your community and relationships with potential customers and collaborators. Live events can include seminars, events at the Chamber of Commerce, black tie affairs, award programs, etc. Any activity that reaches your target market or your peers can be important to building visibility. Attend events often—for the purpose of networking and relationship building. Be sure to include events where you are not on the event committee—not getting an award—not presenting an award—and not a sponsor. Attending live events gives you an opportunity to pass out business cards and focus on getting your name out there. You may already be connected to different organizations and youth programs but I challenge you to get out of the circle you've already made a nest in—and spread your wings. Finding events is not difficult. The internet makes it increasingly easy for you to find your ideal clients on any given day. Turn to your local paper or online sources such as **www.meetup.com** to find happenings in your community. Meetup.com is awesome because you can search for groups based on your interests or location. The purpose of Meetup.com is to "meet" in person as opposed to online—and many meet-up groups get together weekly.

PILLAR CHALLENGE

Get a free account at **www.meetup.com**. In the search box, enter your city or zip code and find groups that interest you. Read more about the group and their past meet-ups. Join at least 3 groups, introduce yourself, and put their next meet-up date on your calendar. Then get out there and connect.

I will talk about event planning in the next chapter but under visibility the focus is on—networking, mingling, getting your name known, passing out business cards, and connecting. A lot of people network but not effectively. Attending events is a great opportunity when you have specific goals in mind. One of those goals is to connect with as many people as possible. Effective relationship building at live events has to do with "how" you connect. Live events are not your opportunity to "water hose" people with what you do. It is not the place to overload people with information about your company or attempt to make a sale. You are there to build relationships and keeping that in mind will allow your business to grow naturally. The more "visible" you are to your potential clients, the better chance you have for the relationship to sprout business in the future. It will be awesome if you can network once a week. I realize you may not have that much time or your locality may not have enough activity for once a week, so although that would be awesome—once a month would be great, and quarterly will work.

VIDEO

The second tool I want to discuss in terms of visibility is video. Attending live events allows your potential clients to see you in person. Video gives your clients an opportunity to see you virtually. Many people struggle with video because they fear being in front of a camera. I must admit—even though I am often on stage speaking to thousands of people—I do not like taking pictures or being on video. So if you're like me, let's conquer this challenge together, ok?

Video is a great marketing and visibility tool because it helps your prospective clients get to know you from a comfortable distance. The video does not have to be long or complicated. Two to four minutes is long enough to share a useful tip or series of tips showcasing your expertise and your willingness to help. But most importantly—let your personality shine through. Then end the video by sending the viewers to your website or social media page where they can get more tips or a free resource. Remember that opt-in box? Make the information in your videos valuable to your viewers and you will grow a list of loyal people anxious to spread the word about your program.

Technology has made video making a very simple concept. Whether you choose an expensive camera or a small, inexpensive one such as the Flip Camera—it is very easy to create video. The Flip Camera has no wires to connect and fits in the palm of your hand so you can shoot video anytime—anyplace. Remember the objective is for your ideal client to get to know you. That means it doesn't have to be in a studio or be perfect—just be you. Putting a weekly video on your website would be very beneficial. You can share your videos on YouTube, Facebook and Twitter—tools I discuss in more detail later. You could also use the videos to make blog posts. The point is, your video needs to be visible because while some prefer to read—others prefer to watch.

> ## TIP
>
> The easiest way to start with video is to create a top ten list. Let's say you have a program helping kids pass the SAT—you could do "The Top 10 Things Kids Can Do to Prepare for the SAT". Then do 10 videos. Each video only need be about 2-4 minutes—keep it short and to the point.

ARTICLE WRITING

The third valuable application for creating visibility is Article Writing. Do not confuse this with blogging, which we discussed in the fourth chapter. Article Writing is when you submit your work to article sharing websites for the online world to see. These websites offer free accounts and allow you to write and submit your articles of choice. The best place to begin is **EzineArticles.com**. The major difference in article writing and blogging is your use of tone and language. Article writing establishes your expertise so writing with a professional tone is crucial. Your potential clients want assurance that you know what you are talking about. Blogging is generally a more relaxed conversation style used to build a relationship with your readers. Be sure to use the help guides and videos offered by websites that accept articles. Just as with making a video—you want to create as many articles as you can. Article writing once a week is advisable but once a month will work. Imagine what your prospective clients will think when you give them a link to articles you have written and published online. Article writing—along with live events and video—have the potential to skyrocket your business by giving you the visibility to establish credibility with potential clients. Consistency and quality of these visibility tools will matter, so if you have the time and the energy—being awesome with all three can be extremely effective. The more you use each avenue the more your program will grow. However, this is not something you can perfect overnight. I suggest you choose two visibility tools to begin with.

SOCIAL MEDIA

One of the best ways to increase your visibility is through social media. Out of all the visibility tools I've shared, the two I want you to master first is Live Events and Social Media. You may already be active in social media but there is a difference between doing it—doing it well—and doing it so it builds your business. Social media can be a lot of fun but it can also be very time consuming unless you have a system. There are hundreds of social media sites. The top 3 that work for me are Facebook, Twitter, and LinkedIn. These three websites—in my opinion— bring the most visibility. All are free but you need to create an account at each site. While based on the same concept—they each vary in style and audience.

- **Facebook.** Setting up a Facebook page for your business is rather simple. Your business page is also called a "fan page." You can make as many business or fan pages as you would like—free of charge. On Facebook, you are required to have a personal profile that links to your business page. This is good in that your potential clients can get to know you—not just your business. On the flip side—your personal actions on Facebook can negatively impact your business. It is important to keep in mind that Facebook is not a place to put a picture of you in a bikini, make the wrong kind of controversial statements or have heated arguments with family members.

Once you create your business page—make sure your brand is clearly displayed. For example, the name of my Facebook page is Empowering Youth for Success— which is also the name of my business. I also have one for the youth called—"Teen Wall of Fame". Lastly, I have a private page for International Association of Youth Empowerment Program members. Your brand needs to remain clear regardless of which social media website you choose to use. Facebook is forever evolving and changing—but knowing your brand when you create the page will alleviate being stuck with a page name you don't want in the future.

The idea behind using a Facebook page for visibility is to connect with people on the internet. At last count, Facebook had 600 million users. At this rate—you will never run out of people to connect with. You can search for people by name which makes connecting with current clients a breeze. You can also search by subject which makes finding potential clients easier. People become a member of your fan page community by pressing the "Like" button and anything you write on your page will go directly to your fans. Facebook makes Marketing and Visibility almost effortless.

✦ **Twitter.** Twitter is hard to grasp for a lot of people and it is very different from Facebook. Many people stray away from using Twitter—simply because it "looks" complicated on initial contact with the website. Once you become more familiar, it is not complicated—and in my experience—can bring more visibility than Facebook. Just as on Facebook, you begin Twitter by opening a free account and completing your profile. You can update your profile as many times as you want on Twitter.

You can also change your name if your brand changes without losing any of your followers. On Twitter you do not have much space to let the world know who you are and what you do—so clarity is critical. Twitter is very similar to sending a text message. If you have teenagers or work with youth—you are familiar with texting. When you send a text, you only have a certain number of characters and then the text field is full. Twitter is not meant to be a long conversation. You have to share your message in 140 characters or less—which includes spaces, periods, and commas. That's enough space to post a quote or send a tip which is the perfect opportunity for sharing your expertise, building relationships and increasing visibility. Therefore, being concise and direct is very important. Otherwise, you are wasting everyone's time.

On Twitter you can search by name or specific topic to find people you want to connect with. You can follow people on Twitter and they can follow you. It is all about being social. Remember, we are working on the "Know, Like, and Trust" factor on Twitter as well. As your potential clients begin to like you—they will become interested in what you do. If you lead with what you do instead of who you are—you will lose people in the social media world. Use social media for visibility without pushing your program or services. Resist the urge to always talk about the services you offer and allow your fans to get to know you. I suggest you take this opportunity to share other people's blog or videos. If potential clients see you as a valuable resource, they will be drawn to you even more. Remember, it's all about relationship building.

✦ **LinkedIn.** This social website is totally different from Facebook and Twitter. It is a more professional environment created for business people. It is not the "chatty" type of network like Facebook and Twitter. LinkedIn is also free but it has a different tone because it began as a place for jobseekers to post résumés. Now, it has turned into a social media site where business people can do business. You should not be as "social" on LinkedIn. It is more professional and commands professional visibility. On LinkedIn, people are interested in your business more than who you are personally.

It is essential that you create a profile on all three social media websites. It will not only increase your visibility with potential clients—but will aide in list building. Recall that we covered list-building in chapter 4. You can give your potential clients the option to "follow" you on each of your social media pages. This, in turn, creates an opportunity for you to invite followers to your website. You can share your social media links on your blog and every time you blog—you also want to share a link to your blog post with your social media friends. Building social media relationships by providing useful information will be very rewarding for your business.

TIP

I highly encourage you to get a free account at **www.Hootsuite.com**. This website allows you to connect to your Facebook, Twitter, and LinkedIn accounts from your Hootsuite page. You can post something on Hootsuite.com and decide on which social media account you want your message to post. You can post your message to all three or just one or two—it's all up to you. Hootsuite also allows you to schedule your posts. This is very helpful when you're at a live event and won't have time to visit your social media pages. Hootsuite gives you the option of scheduling hours, weeks or months in advance. I recommend posting 3-4 times a day to the different social media sites. Instead of sitting in front of your computer posting all day, you can schedule them all at one time. Posting morning, noon and evening—keeps you actively involved in relationship building—and is essential for strong visibility. Consistency in the social media world is a must.

It is also important to pay close attention to *what* you post. Your information needs to be valuable. If people do not find your information valuable, they will either "hide" your messages or delete you from their page. Like blogging, you must be conscious of what you post and post consistency. If you post too often or post what others perceive as junk—you will be deleted or hidden. If you post too sparingly—your potential clients will stop following you because they can't find you. You can create a posting schedule that fits your lifestyle—just be consistent. Once people know your pattern they know what to expect. You don't have to post at the exact same minute every day—it's not that serious. Posting three times a day and having parameters is fine. For example, my followers know I don't do social media on Sunday.

When your followers begin to like you, they will naturally be interested in what you do. But remember—when you lead with what you do instead of who you are—in the Social Media world—you will be toast. If a stranger walks up to you and all of a sudden says—"Hi, I love you. Can we get married right now?"—you would look at them strangely. Well, it's the same at a Live Event and online—with Social Media. People want to get to know you. So please resist the urge to always talk about your stuff or your program. Social media can reap great rewards for your business—when done well.

TIP

Once you start creating different online accounts you will have a lot of usernames and passwords to keep up with. I suggest using RoboForm to securely store all your usernames and passwords. You are going to need a service like this because remembering all those usernames and passwords is impossible! Take my advice. I know all too well how overwhelming it can be.

So, there you have it. You have completed pillar four of the 6 Pillars to Success. I hope you now understand the important of visibility with potential clients. Building relationships is what will make your business prosper. All four tools, when done consistently and done well—will increase your visibility and your business. Every relationship you successfully build is a potential client. How visible are you and your program?

6

Success Pillar #5: Programming

illar number five of the 6 Pillars to Success is Programming. Before I start explaining programming, let's recap what you have learned thus far. Pillar 1 was all about branding. Branding is who you are and what you want to be known for. In the chapter about Clarity you narrowed your focus, identified your target market, and profiled your ideal client. In the third Pillar, you learned about Marketing and how to successfully grow your business. We also talked about your website, list building, and blogging—and the value they have in your marketing strategy. Pillar 4—Visibility—explained how important connecting and building relationships through social media is to your program success. Now, we have reached Pillar 5—Programming. We are continuing to build upon a solid foundation so you can truly be successful in your mission to help more youth.

There are two things I want to say before I jump into Programming.

Number one—people rarely buy only what they need, they spend money on what they want. It is important to sell your clients what they want and give them what they need in the process. Think about what your ideal client wants. This goes back to the WIIFM that I talked about a few chapters back. Clients are increasingly concerned about "What's In It For Me?" They really don't care to know that you have the best tutoring program. They don't really want to hear that you have the best price. That is not what causes people to buy. They want to know how your service is going to benefit them or their child. *Later in this chapter, I'm going to share the top ten reasons people buy.* Even though you operate from your passion and have a difficult time seeing your program as a business—the fact of the matter is that you are selling. You're selling your job skills class. You're selling your mentorship program. You're selling your SAT prep. You're selling your child care services. No matter what you offer—you are in the business of selling. If you focus your marketing on the benefits of your program to your clients and not the service itself—you can successfully answer the WIIFM question and satisfy your markets wants and needs.

Number two—I want you to practice starting with the end in mind. While your strategy is to let your potential clients know the benefits of your program—the ultimate goal is still to sell your program. You have to understand the mindset of why people buy so you know how to make the offer irresistible. Determine your goal for the event—or the program—or the class—or the product you want to sell? Then work backwards. Stop creating *stuff* just because it sounds good to you. Well, of course you can keep doing it that way but you will waste a lot of time, energy, effort and money creating *stuff* your market doesn't want to buy. This is where Clarity and Programming do the tango.

There are four general areas I want to focus on regarding Programming. They are increasing participation, event planning, programs and services, and operating systems. I will cover three of the four areas briefly and then explain in detail the one I feel is most important to programming. Developing programs tailored to your ideal client is essential to a growing business. Pillar #5 also happens to my strongest area of expertise.

INCREASING PARTICIPATION

Increasing the participation in your program is really and truly rooted in the success of everything we have worked on to this point. The reason you are not having the participation you deserve is possibly because you have not identified the correct target market and you have not created your ideal client. When you speak to the general population—no one knows you are talking to them. The problem also could be your branding. If you are presenting the wrong image, or an image different from what you offer—people are confused. A confused mind doesn't buy. Perhaps you are having a problem with visibility because you are not hanging out in the right online and offline places. If you're not sharing your information where your target market hangs out– they won't know you exist. You could have a marketing problem—which means your message is not clear or perhaps you're not providing a place for prospects to come— and build the know, like and trust factor.

Can you see why you must have the other pillars in place? The increasing participation topic is a great opportunity for you to see how the pillars work together—and why branding and clarity have to be right—in order for everything else in your program to travel the direction of success. If you put the pillars into action—you won't have to worry about increasing program participation. It will come naturally as a result of having a good solid foundation.

EVENT PLANNING

Event planning is very similar to increasing participation when it comes to the programming pillar. If you successfully build your business using the 6 Pillars to Success—you will undoubtedly not have a problem with event attendance. In event planning, it is really important to know what your market wants and pay attention to *how* you market. Whether it's a workshop, conference, lock-in or parent meeting—parents are not going to show up just because it's a good idea or a worthy cause. Anything that takes a parent out of their way or adds to an already busy schedule is not going to be as successful as you may expect. You have to give parents a reason to come out of the house after they've worked all day or to get up early on a Saturday to attend your seminar or to bring their child to a lock and pick them up at six in the morning. What is in it for the parents? It doesn't always matter that it will benefit their child.

TIP

Hosting an annual event that your company becomes known for is a great way to increase visibility and attendance. People who know and love your products or services will start to plan their schedule around your event every year.

OPERATING SYSTEM

Having steady and consistent program income is very important. You don't want to be on a rollercoaster when it comes to income. But if you continue to fly by the seat of your pants when operating your program—you will experience up and down success. If you don't create operating systems that work— you are building a business that will soon imprison you. You're doing everything yourself so you can't take vacation. You can't leave the building without your cell phone for fear of something happening that only you can handle. Your business will control your life and everything you do. Your program will become a ball and chain—and that is not what you want. You want a business where you can train someone and easily delegate tasks. I often hear youth-serving entrepreneurs, CEO's, directors, etc. say . . .

"Well, I don't have time to train somebody."

"I can do it myself a whole lot faster than the time it's going to take me to train someone else."

"I just know how to do it. I don't know how to tell somebody else to do it."

"No one is going to do it the way I want it done."

These are all horrible scenarios upon which to build a business. Here's the thing. When you have a youth-serving program, you have the program because you want to help youth. Not just this year or for the next five years. Your service will likely be needed for the next 100 years; therefore, you need to set your program up so when you decide to—retire, sit back, and sip Shirley Temples—your legacy will continue to empower youth for success.

The key to creating operating systems that will set your program up longevity and make life easier for you—is to write things down. Write down everything you do in conducting day to day business. Write how to do it, what steps to take, and how long it takes. Your business practices need to be such that someone can step right in, pick it up, and continue to make it a success. Plus, the entire point of 6 Pillars to Success is for your business to grow. If it grows like you and I expect—you need good operating systems in place for your new staff to follow. When you are in a decision making capacity—the joy of growing a business is often replaced with the duties of operating, managing, and overseeing. I have helped clients who unfortunately worked themselves into such a corner they had to shut their program down in order to put operating systems in place. Is this what you want? Putting good operating systems in your business *now* is key to successful programming and steady growth. I realize trying to remember all the steps for everything you do can be a daunting thought. The next time you have to complete a task—grab a piece of paper or an audio recorder or video camera and document your steps *as* you go through them. Before you know it you will have systems written for everything.

PILLAR CHALLENGE

Write a step-by-step outline for enrolling a new child/parent in your program. Start with the inquiry phone call. When do you answer the telephone? How do you want the telephone to be answered? What do you tell the caller? Do you tell them a little and then send them information? When do you invite them to visit? What about when a parent comes to your building, what is your process? Do you talk to them first and then take them for a tour. Do you give them a brochure when they leave? When do you give them registration forms? Write down every step of the enrollment process.

DEVELOPING PROGRAMS AND SERVICES

Developing programs and services is what drives your business. This is the reason your program exists. You are developing products or services to *sell* to your potential clients. The very first thing you must realize when it comes to developing programs and services—is that you cannot do everything. You cannot offer every program and service under the sun and expect to be successful. I recommend you begin with two programs until you get a firm grasp on your business. Why? When you are trying to sustain and grow your business—you need to be focused. Offering too many things at one time can be confusing for you and your potential clients. Remember, a confused mind does not buy. Offering more than three programs, products, or services will cause confusion. With confusion comes zero decisions and without a decision—you make zero dollars. Research has shown it best to only offer two things—"no" is already a built in third option. However, if you focus on your branding and what your target market wants—narrowing your offerings to two will not be difficult. If you have a really hard time putting a service on the back burner—I understand—I have to grow through this process too but it's just a cycle and it won't be the last time you put great ideas on hold for the sake of long-term success. Look at it this way—if you can continue to offer the same three services forever—guess what, you're business is not growing. For now, choose two services and build them as solid as a rock. Once you have an established business and people know your program—you can evaluate increasing the number of services you offer.

From these two programs, you will choose a foundation program. Your foundation program is the service you are going to build your entire business, program, and reputation on. When somebody thinks of you, this is the service you want them to think of. Your foundation program is who you are and what you stand for. It's your core—your money maker. This is what I consider your bread and butter.

There is quite a process to creating a foundation program and it will take a great deal of your time and effort. A good way to begin creating your foundation program is to determine what you would choose if your program could only offer one service for the rest of your life. This is the easiest way I know to reach the true core of why your business exists and identify your foundation program. Of course, before you select the program and start trying to market—it is beneficial to know why people buy in the first place. Without paying customers—all you have is a hobby.

7 REASONS WHY PEOPLE BUY

The ultimate goal for having a business is so people will pull out their wallets. If you do not understand why people buy you cannot effectively use the 6 Pillars to lead your prospective client down the road to purchasing your service or program.

> **Number 1.** People always want something in return for their effort and hard work and the easier it is to get— the better they like it. If you have a program or product that will help your client gain or profit—you have an opportunity for them to buy from you. You can offer something additional that your parent doesn't have to pay for like a bonus, freebie or discount. While your customer benefits from the gain—you can build the expense into your operating costs.

PILLAR STUDY

Let's say you have a child care program and you provide meals, transportation and the kids learn computer. A parent will be more likely to sign up if you quote a flat $200 tuition rate and say it includes transportation, meals, snacks, supplies, and computer class. That is more appealing than saying—*the tuition is $50 a week and the transportation is $20 a week and breakfast is $25 and lunch is $55 and snack is $15, and the computer program is $35.* They may both total $200 but the feeling for the parent will be much different.

✦ **Number 2.** People buy because they need security. People will go through great lengths to prevent losing something. They do not want to lose property, time, or anything else. The fear of loss and the need for security is one of the biggest motivators for buying. If you offer a program, a product, or services that can help parents or clients feel more secure now or in the future—they are more likely to buy. You can share how your program will positively impact their child's future thereby giving parents a certain level of security knowing they are preparing their child for success. Example: You can share that your SAT prep class is designed to get their child into the college they really want to attend instead of settling for their 2nd, 3rd, 4th, or 5th choice. Or you can share how your program will save the parents the expense of four or five SAT retakes. Or save the parents money on application fees and lost sleep worrying if their child will be accepted. Anything that has to do with avoiding loss will be a purchase trigger.

✦ **Number 3.** Another reason people choose to buy goods and services is the pride of ownership. They want to be noticed or recognized. Adults are the same as kids. While they refuse to admit it—many adults buy things because of the attention it gets them. This is the reason you see so many people driving expensive cars and joining elite country clubs. Adults enjoy "status". This can be very beneficial in the youth-serving world as well. You can use this trigger to enroll parents and increase your program participation by offering something exclusive. One specific way to build in "status" is by having an application process. When you position your program as exclusive or difficult to get into—potential clients see it as an opportunity to be special. Whether it's the name you choose for your program or specific classes you offer—have a process the parent must go through to enter. Yes, I know you want them to enroll. I know you need them to enroll. I know you may be facing layoffs, closure or taking a J-O-B if someone doesn't enroll in your program quickly but when you position your program as something they have to jump through some hoops to get into—you will be amazed how it increases your business. Exclusivity will cause a parent to drive past the free program down the street and beat down your door to pay for your program. The human need to be noticed is a great opportunity for business growth.

Number 4. People buy because they have an interest in doing something easier or more efficiently. Do you have a way to promote your product, program, or service as something that's going to make life easier for the parent or the child? If so, you absolutely want to include that benefit in your direct and indirect marketing. A parent is more likely to choose your program if you can make life easier for them. For example: offer a home study version of your SAT prep course or offer transportation from the child's school. Now the parent doesn't have to think about how to get their child to you and get their child home. Whatever you offer—there's lots of ways to make things easier for the customer.

✦ **Number 5.** People buy because of their desire for excitement or pleasure. This is a very interesting trigger because excitement and pleasure doesn't seem to go with purchasing. This is especially true if the purchase is going to be large. However, people desire excitement in their lives. They desire things that are pleasing to the eye and make them feel good. Let's say you have a ballet school or cheerleading gym. Well, offering ballet lessons three times a week is great—but have you noticed most ballet schools have a recital? The reason they have a recital is to build excitement. They're keeping the kids excited because they are going to perform and they're keeping the parents excited because they love to see their kids perform. All that excitement keeps the children enrolled and the parents paying. No matter what kind of program you have—there is a way to add a component that keeps the parents and the kids excited. It could be a spelling bee. It could be a holiday program. It could be a graduation. What can you do to add excitement?

FREEZE

Be sure to talk about your exciting event on social media, on your blog and you can even do a press release.

✦ **Number 6.** Clients also buy for reasons of self-improvement or an increase in effectiveness. Your investment of both money and time in this book is a good example of your desire to improve your program and increase its effectiveness. Everyone wants and needs to improve or be more efficient. You have to tell the market why your program is going to improve their child's SAT score. Use marketing and visibility to let potential clients know how your program is more effective.

You also need to know your competition—what they offer—and how they offer it. Not so you can copy them but so you can do something different or possibly fill a need your competition doesn't. Let your potential clients know what sets you apart. Without bad mouthing your competition, make it clear why your program is better.

Number 7. The last reason people buy is the desire for importance or the need to feel appreciated. Humans need to feel accepted, appreciated and like we are making a difference. Most people are starving for acceptance and appreciation so if you have programs or services that can satisfy this need—your business can be highly successful. Letting your potential clients know you donate a percentage of the parent payments to XYZ charity will make them feel they are helping others when they buy from you. Donating to charities can help meet your very own need to feel appreciated and also give your potential buyers a reason to choose your service over other similar services. Haven't you purchased something because a portion of it was going to help a charity? It's a huge trigger for all of mankind.

Look for ways to increase participation in your program and plan events that will get your program known throughout your market. When building a successful youth-serving program—you must be willing to serve your potential customers before they will respond with loyalty. Proper programming—along with the other pillars—can help you build a strong business that will continue to grow. After all, if your program is not strong how can you empower young people for success?

7

Success Pillar #6: Sustainability

You have now learned almost everything you need to make your youth-serving business a success. Hold on—before you celebrate—we still have one last pillar to go through. Pillar six in the 6 Pillars to Success is Sustainability.

Now that you have selected two services and your foundation program, we can journey on to Sustainability. This is all about creating a plan to sustain your business once the other pillars are successfully in place. You have been laying an awesome foundation since Pillar One—getting clear on your target market and identifying your ideal client. You learned that once you are clear on your ideal client, marketing becomes easier because you know who your program is trying to attract. Then you learned to have visibility with your target market and how social media is important for building relationships—which moved you to working on programming. By now you should *really* see how all of these pieces fit to achieve the success your dreams are made of.

For a sustainable business you must have a plan. If you don't have a plan in place to keep your program growing, all that I've shared will be useless. There will be no point to the first five pillars because six months from now you will have the same problems. What I want to impress upon you the most throughout this chapter is that you cannot rely on grant funding, donations, parent payments or fish fry dinners to grow and sustain your program. The entire point of 6 Pillars to Success is so you can finally stop worrying about the money and start focusing on empowering youth.

In this chapter, I will cover four strategies for program sustainability. Let me warn you—this pillar will probably take you the furthest away from your comfort zone—but I know you can handle it. The four areas are product creation, affiliate sales, coaching-consulting, and adding additional services. Exploring and utilizing these avenues can help sustain your growing business. Let's talk about the many things you can do outside of and in addition to your primary service to bring money into your program.

COACHING AND CONSULTING

Coaching and consulting is a strong opportunity for business sustainability. If you have chosen to open a business offering a particular service—you are likely very confident in the knowledge you have in that area. Using your knowledge, there are ways to take your business to another level and generate additional money for the program. Never underestimate the knowledge you have. It can be a powerful tool. I encourage you to sit down and write a list of your skills and abilities. What are you good at? Without jeopardizing your brand—what can you offer your potential clients outside of how you currently serve them? Coaching and Consulting is a way to take your skills and bump them up to something that either your market will want to buy or that can branch off into a second market. Let's say you tutor kids after school and on the weekends. You could consult on starting and running a tutoring business. Even if you're brand new—there's always someone who is newer than you. Even if you only know a little—there is always a group of people who know nothing. The things that seem easy to you are not easy to everyone.

Perhaps you can turn your knowledge into a curriculum, product, or program that can be available for other youth-serving organizations to purchase. This is an example of taking something you know and turning it into what is called *multiple streams of income.* Come up with some type of class, a lesson, or a program you can create from your existing knowledge—then place it for sale on your website and let your website do the rest of the work for you. This way—even if you are not "working"— your product is still generating income. I like knowing that even when I am asleep—my 6 Pillars to Success course—is helping youth-serving programs and generating income so I can empower more youth. This is the value of bringing your business to an online environment and the benefits are endless.

PILLAR STUDY

I have a youth entrepreneurship program called "How To Start a Business Even if You're A Kid". I had been teaching youth entrepreneurship classes in person for 20 years and just like you—I was the offline brick and mortar person. That's all I knew. So when I expanded my business online, I had to find a way to translate my face-to-face class to a virtual learning program. Now, instead of limiting kids by physical attendance—Youth Success Academy was born and is literally available to any child in the world with email access. But then I turned the academy into a step-by-step curriculum that other youth-serving programs can purchase and facilitate with their students. Even if it's 2 o'clock in the morning and I am fast asleep—a parent can go on to www.EmpoweringYouthforSuccess.com and enroll their child in the Youth Success Academy or youth-serving program can go to www.IAYEP.com and purchase one of my courses. So I've taken something I originally saw as a classroom business and turned my knowledge into *multiple streams of income*. And you can do that too!

Another example of how you can use your knowledge to work for you is to create an e-book (electronic book) and make it available online for purchase. E-books maybe a new concept for you but people are now buying e-books and downloading them to their computer instead of purchasing a hard-copy from the bookstore. This is a direct result of today's "I want it now" mentality. If someone is online searching for information about how to start a tutoring business they want answers now so when they come across your e-book called "How to Start a Tutoring Business in 5 Easy Steps"—they don't want to wait for the book to arrive in six to eight weeks. An e-book is awesome because people can purchase and download it immediately. They can open the book on their computer and read it or they can print it. But it's an awesome opportunity for you and very beneficial for your business. Having multiple streams of income will give your business sustainability and an e-book is just another way youth-serving programs can get in the game.

PILLAR CHALLENGE

Choose a class, a lesson, or a program you can create from knowledge you already have or an activity you are currently doing—and translate it into something that can be purchased and delivered online.

PRODUCT CREATION

Coaching, consulting, and product creation really go together. The key is not to be content with offering a product or service in just one way. Whether it's coaching clients, offering classes, writing a book, doing a webinar, or a teleseminar—you can add multiple streams of income to your youth-serving business. There is always a way to kick things up to the next level. It will take dedication on your part but in the end you will have a business that can sustain itself—even if enrollment is down and funding ceases.

FREEZE

You can create ways to generate money for your program even when you are on vacation. You just have to know what to do and how to do it.

PILLAR STUDY

You will be surprised. The 6 Pillars to Success was developed as a result of questions people asked me over and over and over again. Their questions were phrased differently but I found myself repeating the same answers. I realized I could help a lot more youth-serving executives if I did a class and once I wrote down all of the information I was sharing—it fell into six categories. I did not wake up and say—*I'm going to write something on 6 Pillars to Success.* No! Remember, I talked about starting at the end and working backwards. I didn't have the pillars already. I came up with the category titles after I grouped my answers and realized what they had in common. So then I had 6 categories but still no name for the class. If you've been following me for any amount of time, you know the class originally had a different name. Silly me—I tried to come up with some cool fancy name that didn't resonate with my market. *Learn from my mistake and keep it simple.*

I created what turned out to be a six week class which I am sure you can imagine after reading this book. I could have stopped there and offer the 6 week class every three months—but there was more to uncover. *I'm sharing these details so when you go back and look at what you have and want to create—you can learn from the process I went through.* So I recorded each of the 6 sessions and turned it into a product that can be purchased from my website any time of the day or night. The course goes much deeper into the 6 Pillars than I can in this book and has handouts and templates to assist with implementation.

So that's level number two. Then I realized people spend a lot of time in the car so in addition to the digital version of the 6 Pillars to Success course, I offer 6 physical CDs with an action guide. That gives me yet another opportunity to sell this program in my sleep. But I'm not done.

Level number three. During the 6 Pillars to Success course, you will learn everything you need to put the pillars in place. I give lots of great handouts and bonuses to help. But not everyone will have the skills to get it done. Some people will get stuck on a certain pillar.

Some people need the accountability—or they'll get busy—or they'll procrastinate. Some people want to ask questions and get feedback as they put the pillars in place. And that's where Phase Two of the 6 Pillars to Success comes into play. GPS to Success provides live group coaching/consulting to help you implement the pillars every step of the way. You also have the option of Passport to Success which is private coaching/consulting to *get it done*. Then I offer a Done For You option for people who don't have time or care not to do the work themselves. Plus there are four more levels—but for the sake of time I think you get the idea. You can do the same exact thing over—and over—and over—and over again.

I bet you've figured out that the 6 Pillars to Success is my foundation program.

AFFILIATE SALES

Having affiliate sales can also help your business achieve sustainability. You may be unfamiliar with this terminology and would understand if I said referral or commission. Those are two words offline people know very well. Most businesses depend on referrals and with affiliate sales—if you tell someone about a particular product or program and they purchase—you get a commission. It is really that simple. My program is set up so that once you join my mailing list or buy anything from me—you automatically get an affiliate number. By using your affiliate number to recommend my products or services you get a 25% commission on every sale you initiate.

Choose carefully the products and services you recommend; you do not want to be an affiliate for everyone in the world. Only recommend things you believe in. Do not let money be your only reason for recommending a product or service. Affiliate sales are an easy way to bring another stream of income your way—however, if people feel you are recommending the product or service only for money—your integrity will be questioned. Integrity is always the master of success. By recommending any and everything—your business could really suffer. I encourage you to only be an affiliate for products and services you have tried or trust. Your reputation is on the line.

I personally use affiliate sales to help recommend the products and services I think will help the parents, youth and youth organizations I serve. My clients appreciate that I have suggested resources listed on my website. It is not all about the money. I also recommend people who don't have an affiliate program. I am trying to help my clients and that should be your number one goal in affiliate sales. While you may recommend a product or service—the final decision is left up to the buyer. You are not responsible for refunds or product support. Do you see how affiliate sales work? Using this properly can add an additional level to sustaining your business. Just be careful not to go overboard—an affiliate sale is not worth a jeopardized image and the success of your business.

ADDITIONAL SERVICES

There are many ideas for adding additional income opportunities to your business or program. The one in particular I want to discuss will help you in all of the pillars but is especially crucial in sustainability—is getting testimonials about your programs or services. A testimonial is when a customer says positive things about your program or product and you use what they've said on your website, registration page, or even the back cover of your book. Testimonials can be helpful to your business in two ways. First, by using your customers' words to promote your business. When someone gives a good testimonial about your program, get as much use out of that testimonial as you can. Consumers want to see honest reviews from others who have tried your product or service. When I am making a buying decision I always look at the testimonials to see what others think.

Be sure you get good testimonials. If your program is good, you should not have a problem. Testimonials will be a little difficult in the beginning when your program is new but they will come. A good way to get testimonials when you are starting out is to ask for volunteers to test and rate your product or service. Select two or three people and allow them to read your e-book and give you a testimonial. Do not direct them to give a positive testimonial—but to give an honest one. Testimonials can also reaffirm that your product will appeal to your target market. You may have to let two or three people go through your class for free to gather testimonials. Whatever it takes, testimonials will help sell your program.

> ## FREEZE
> Do not give away more than three for free just to gain testimonials.

Testimonials can be used online and offline. If you have a brochure or flyer—put a testimonial on it. When prospective buyers don't know you—they are looking for ways to validate choosing your service. If a customer says your program is great, this is confirmation for them. Why not utilize the back of your business card? For many people, it's just wasted space. Consider adding a testimonial from a client. Testimonials are an awesome way to build "know, like, and trust".

Second, by giving testimonials for other people. It is equally important that you *give* testimonials for the products and services of others. This is a great way to get free advertising and connect your program to other successful business leaders. I am always looking for opportunities to do testimonials because I enjoy supporting other people. While many think it could hinder your business—it actually really helps. When a testimonial is given for my program—I also get a picture of the client, their web address, name, and phone number. Every time I use the testimonial, I may not list all of the contact information but I always include their name and their website. Online testimonials give you visibility and also give visibility to the person making the testimonial. The back cover of a book is a perfect place for testimonials because everyone reads the back of the book before they purchase it. Did you read the testimonials on the back of this book? Did you visit Nicki or Al's website to learn more about their business? That's visibility.

If I receive hundreds of testimonials, I have to go through and pick a few that I think effectively promotes my business. I can't use them all so it is important to know how to do a testimonial correctly. When giving a testimonial—you want it to be amazing. Remember, clients look at testimonials when making their buying decision—so give the best review possible. Giving testimonials has really paid off for me. I can't tell you how many people I have met and connected with because of a video or written testimonial showcased on someone's website. When creating testimonials—whether video or written—try to make your testimonial stand out. If you need help in creating one—visit www.IAYEP.com and read the testimonials some of my clients have written. You can get good ideas about writing a testimonial that will be used.

PILLAR CHALLENGE

When you are finished reading this book, write or video tape a testimonial and email it to **testimonial@iayep.com**. Don't forget to include your contact information and a photo; you may be featured in the next book or on my website.

Once you have your business established—sustainability is not that difficult—it is simply transforming your skills, abilities and knowledge. It begins with clarity and knowing exactly what to offer your ideal client and ends with an arsenal of products, programs or services that will effectively sustain your business. The 6 Pillars to Success have worked for me and with focus, time, and effort—you can achieve extraordinary program success too.

8

Conclusion

efore we officially end I want to make something clear. Many times, I have trouble convincing my coaching clients that their youth-serving program is really a business. Even if you're a government agency that serves youth— you are still running a business. So the faster you become comfortable with that, the six pillars to success will not be as difficult to implement. I also want to emphasize that even if you are a non-profit business or organization—it is okay to make money. It is okay to have a goal of being a successful business.

Passion is great. You need passion in order to have staying power but "Passion Won't Pay The Bills." Whether you are a brand new business or you've been in business for quite some time, the 6 Pillars can take your program to the next level and improve sustainability.

The first pillar I discussed was Branding. Youth-Serving Executives are missing it when it comes to branding. When I say branding, I am referring to your ability to create a consistent image that your prospective customers will remember and recognize. If they need your services, you will immediately come to mind. It takes time, work, and consistency to build a brand. There is a major difference in naming a business and building a brand. In the GPS to Success program, you will learn how to choose a name that says exactly what you do and who you are.

Pillar two is Clarity. Clarity is defining your focus. It helps you understand what your clients want and need so can give them exactly what they are looking for. What is your business focus? Most of my coaching is spent on these first two pillars because they are the foundation of your business. Clarity is the true foundation. Everything you do in your business is built from Clarity. When you get crystal clear on the services you offer you can begin building a strong and successful business. You have to be clear who you want to work with and what your business does. You can't to do everything. Make decisions about what you do in your business because you *want* to do them, not because it can increase cash flow.

Pillar number three is Marketing. Marketing will grow your business by creating buzz and making sure the right people see your message. You can never do too much marketing; however, you can do the wrong kind of marketing. There are businesses that still spend an enormous amount of money on yellow page ads—which in my opinion—is not a good marketing strategy for youth-serving programs. In 20 years, I have never had a client say they found me in the yellow pages. Also, tools and techniques used by other business cannot be used in the same way with the youth-serving market. Knowing how to market your program will determine your business success.

Pillar number four—Visibility is how you are connecting with your ideal client. You want to always be on the mind of your current and prospective clients. For youth-serving businesses visibility is often a challenge. You may be active in the community but you are not visible online. I challenge you to increase your visibility by going outside of your box and getting online. Online and offline visibility is critical to your program success. Clients want to explore your website and the services you offer. Neither having a website nor utilizing other online opportunities can hinder your growth.

The next pillar we discussed was Programming—which is my favorite area. Having been a youth-serving business owner and working with my coaching clients—I see over and over and over again the number one challenge—there's more competition for the same money. Whether you have paying parents, you get grant funding, you do fundraisers, you seek donations, or you get subsidy payments from a government agency—it's getting harder. People are being much more cautious with their donations and fundraisers are getting harder and harder to sell. Parents who have lost their jobs are not using as many youth services because they don't have the need or the money. Offering services that excite will keep the grant funders anxious to fund you, donators anxious to donate, and parents anxious to pay for your program. The 6 Pillars to Success can help you create programs that have a waiting list.

Lastly, pillar number six is Sustainability. By this point, all the hard work has been done. Sustainability helps your business grow and keeps you from getting "stuck" during hard times. Sustainability is essentially having multiple streams of income. It's about identifying a service you can sell as a new product or as a side to your core business. Do not wait for your funding to dry up or for the economy to go down before you look for alternatives to your business success.

I have enjoyed traveling this journey with you. Take what you have learned and apply the pillars to your business today. It will take time and dedication but you have the information you need to make it happen. I encourage you to go through each pillar again for complete understanding. While this may seem overwhelming—hang in there. It is possible to make money on purpose *and* run a heart-centered youth-serving program! I am a living example of how you can be successful following the 6 Pillars to Success system.

About the Author

Linette Daniels is a national speaker, author and success strategist who, for the past 20 years, has empowered youth from the cradle through college in a variety of youth-serving arenas to include public school, child care, foster care, juvenile court, social services, and early intervention.

As a single parent, she raised 12 therapeutic foster care and 2 biological children using her vision to see infants' progress into developmentally strong toddlers, academically prepared preschoolers, empowered youth and successful adults.

As CEO of Empowering Youth For Success, Inc., she is on a mission to see youth all over the world excel in business, master money and be great leaders so they can create the life they want to live.

As founder of the International Association of Youth Empowerment Programs (IAYEP), Dr. Daniels' is passionate about coaching the Growth, Programming & Sustainability of Youth-Serving Programs because she believes that given the right space, tools, and training; ALL youth can succeed.

Linette Daniels has had the pleasure of a variety of experiences to your benefit, which include:

✦ Mentoring for Big Brothers/Big Sisters and the Boys & Girls Club

✦ Serving as a Court Appointed Special Advocate (CASA) for juvenile court

✦ Serving as Parent-Teacher Association (PTA) Vice President

✦ Serving on the Boards of Head Start and Parks & Recreation

✦ Serving on the Youth Task Force

✦ Facilitating the Strengthening Families Program and the Healthy Families Program

✦ Teaching youth empowerment programs in youth entrepreneurship, life skills and character education**

✦ Facilitating parenting workshops

✦ Consulting for new and seasoned youth-serving programs**

AND

✦ Operating a 24 hour/7 day-a-week regulated family day home

✦ Operating a 24 hour/7 day-a-week licensed childcare center

✦ Director of a privately owned childcare center

- Director of a church run childcare center

- Preschool teacher

- Kindergarten teacher

- Certifying family day home providers

- Childcare instructor at a state university

- Early Intervention Service Coordinator

- Childcare Specialist for a state regulating authority

- 3-hr seminar presenter at the National Association for Educating Young Children (NAEYC) Conference

- Trainer for Early Educators and School-Age Teachers

- Adjunct Faculty for Aspen University (CDA, Associates and Bachelors in Early Childhood Education)**

- National, state and local conference presenter & keynote speaker**

**Current activities

WHEW! LINETTE DANIELS REALLY HAS BEEN THERE & DONE THAT!!!!!

If that's not enough and it's credentials you need:

- A **Bachelors** Degree in Psychology

- A **Masters** Degree in Human Services—Executive Leadership

- **PhD** in Education—Training & Performance Improvement (ABD)

About Empowering Youth For Success (EYS)

EYS focuses on preparing youth for business, financial and leadership success so they can create the life they want to live.

"I believe that given the right space, tools and training; ALL youth can succeed!"

Here's what EYS has to offer:

OUR MISSION

✦ To Empowe.r Youth For **Business, Financial and Leadership Success.**

OUR VISION

✦ To see infants' progress into developmentally strong toddlers, academically prepared preschoolers, empowered youth and successful adults.

OUR PLAN

✦ To provide youth with the skills, knowledge and resources to create the life you want to live.

OUR SERVICES

We offer two programs for youth.

✦ **Youth Success Academy**, the best place on the Internet for youth to become strong, prepared, empowered and successful. Now youth can attend our financial, business and leadership success programs no matter where they live in the world.

✦ **The Bookbag Entrepreneur Club**, an interactive monthly webinar for youth entrepreneurs designed to support their business growth with ongoing training, tips, tools and resources.

The Youth Success Team also travels extensively **speaking** to youth, parents, educators and mentors at colleges & universities, various conferences, award programs, school assemblies, leadership groups, and more.

In addition, **the EYS store** hosts a variety of audio & visual programs, books, games and youth success paraphernalia.

To learn more about EYS, visit
www.EmpoweringYouthForSuccess.com

About the International Association of Youth Empowerment Programs (IAYEP)

Research shows that young people often spend more awake hours each day in youth-serving programs than they do with their parents, as such IAYEP shows youth-serving executives how to build a strong foundation of growth, programming and sustainability so you can **empower more youth.**

OUR MISSION

✦ To empower the **Growth, Programming & Sustainability** of youth-serving programs.

OUR VISION

✦ To see youth-serving programs build a **strong financial foundation**.

OUR PLAN

✦ To show Youth-Serving Leaders "how" to **build a heart-centered program that also makes money** so you can focus on empowering youth.

✦ To provide Youth-Serving Leaders with the tools needed to **Empower Youth For Business, Financial and Leadership Success.**

OUR SIGNATURE PROGRAMS

✦ **Passion Won't Pay The Bills** uses the 6 Pillars to Success to show youth-serving leaders how to have a youth empowerment program that is **thriving**, instead of a vision for youth that is **barely surviving**. Whether you choose the virtual teleclass, the home study course, group coaching, or private strategy sessions; Passion Won't Pay The Bills is a must have for growth, programming and sustainability.

✦ **Empowerpreneurs** is the ultimate youth-adult partnership designed to empower youth entrepreneurs whose business, in turn, provides office and technical support to the youth-serving program. During the Empowerpreneur program, youth learn how to start and run a business, and are given the skills and resources to implement and manage the 6 Pillars to Success.

To learn more about the association, visit **www.IAYEP.com**

Other Books from EYS Publishing

Coming Soon

How to Start A Business Just For Kids

Empowering Youth For Business Success:
10 Keys to Teaching Kids to Excel In Business

Empowering Youth For Financial Success:
10 Keys to Teaching Kids to How to Master Money

Empowering Youth For Leadership Success:
10 Keys to Teaching Kids to Be Great Leaders

What Others are Saying

"For the past several months I have been working closely with Linette Daniels on helping me improve my business. I've been a college recruiter for a very long time and I was looking for ways to enhance my overall business. I thought I knew everything when it came to college recruiting and business in general but when I met Linette Daniels, everything I thought I knew about business changed. Her coaching ideas are simply amazing. This has been one of the best investments I've made in quite some time. I just thought a business coach was someone who worked with corporate America; I was wrong. A business coach such as Linette Daniels can open up your eyes to many incredible opportunities. Her easy-going style of communicating is incredible; whether we're having phone conversations or using the latest technology such as Skype, Linette Daniels is a true professional. The time I spent with her would sometimes be up to 3 hours. I could talk with her all day. She simply gives you so much information and resources that will keep you busy for days and weeks. As a former college and professional basketball player, I understand how critical it is to have a good coach and now it's even more important in the business world.

Having an outstanding business coach on the level of Linette Daniels has truly helped me in all aspects of my business. Because of her incredible talents, I am improving on my business as a college recruiter every day. Her ideas and suggestions enable me to conduct business in a different way and in a more professional way. More importantly, I'm able to bring in new business.

Simply put, Linette Daniels has been a valuable resource for me!"

Al Woods, www.woodsrecruiting.com

"Ms. Daniels has given me valuable information on the importance of zeroing in on my target market, advertising tools and the program that I am the most passionate about, which is, The Leaders of Today Mentoring Program. She has taught me not to diversify my energy and time into activities that do not connect back to my Leaders of Today Mentoring Program. She has given me tools of attraction that have been low to no cost, but the return has been priceless. Ms. Daniels has also increased the visibility of my organization through her contacts that participated in the Entrepreneurs Success Builders Network – The Power of Thought Fundraising Event; Outstanding Youth on the Move and her personal organization, Empowering Youth for Success.

Ms. Daniels is my mentor and now my friend. I look forward to her continual assistance, training and nurturing of my life and business ventures so I will maintain my upward mobility."

Baron Howard, www.bsmartesbn.com

"As an author and professional key note speaker, I empower individuals from various socioeconomic and professional backgrounds in developing a CA$H ONLY mindset and using wise financial principles. One of the vital components to event planning is vision and guidance. Linette Daniels is dynamic in calculated preparation and process. She resonates with wisdom on realistic and practical means to implement strategies. She is a breath of fresh air and she can tell you in which direction the wind is blowing. I had many ideas when I started working with her but now I am getting a clear step-by-step plan on how to make my vision a success."

Deborah Francis, www.cashonlyproductions.com

"My Be True Be U program provides tools and skill sets to help teen girls grow confidently into womanhood by embracing their own truths. Having a heart-centered business is often challenging because the need is so great. I was in the process of restructuring my program when I met Linette. Through working with Linette, I was able to shift my focus from a place of overwhelm and focus on the heartbeat of my business; my vision, purpose and clarity."

Melanie Foote-Davis, www.livebydesigncoaching.com

"Before I met Linette Daniels, I was trading hours for dollars and my business was not positioned for long-term sustainability. After completing her 6 Pillars to Success program, I was more confident in my skills and my business was rebirthed on a firm foundation.

The three things that I learned from Linette are how to create a signature program, demonstrate the value of my service, and increase the visibility of my business. With this information, I have been able to focus on my core values and develop a strategy to help more teens succeed."

Nicki Sanders, www.theteentoolbox.com

Recommended Resources

A Successful Business Relies Upon Great Tools! Here are some to get you started.

- **www.IAYEP.com/gift** A FREE gift for just visiting the association website

- **www.EmpoweringYouthForSuccess.com** Empowering Youth For Success

- **www.IAYEP.com/book-testimonial** To submit a testimonial for this book

- **www.IAYEP.com/samplesurvey** A sample survey you can use as a model

- **www.meetup.com** Great place to find local groups and live events

+ **www.linetterecommends.com/passwordsafe**   Great tool for keeping track of all those usernames and passwords.

+ **www.linetterecommends.com/hosting** Great low-cost website hosting service.

+ **www.linetterecommends.com/autoresponder** Great low cost service for communicating with current and prospective clients.

+ **www.linetterecommends.com/domains** Great place to buy your website domain name.

+ **www.linetterecommends.com/fileshare** Great online service for sharing large files.

+ **www.linetterecommends.com/onlinebackup** Great service for online hard drive backup.

+ **www.PayPal.com**   Low-cost option for sending and receiving money.

+ **www.Hootsuite.com** A tool for managing your social media accounts.

+ **www.Gmail.com** The only free email provider you should use when you have a business.

+ **www.Skype.com** A tool for communicating via chat, phone and video to people all over the world.

+ **www.EzineArtcles.com** The number one site for submitting your original articles.

+ **www.Twitter.com** The top "micro-blogging" social media site.

✦ **www.Facebook.com** The top "social" social media site.

✦ **www.LinkedIn.com** The top "professional" social media site.

✦ **www.YouTube.com** The top "video" social media site.

✦ **www.avast.com/free-antivirus-download** A free option for antivirus software. Going without virus protection is not an option.

CPSIA information can be obtained at www.ICGtesting.com
261883BV00002B/12/P